ART AND COUNTERFEIT

PLATE I—Frontispiece

Fig. 1

Fig. 2

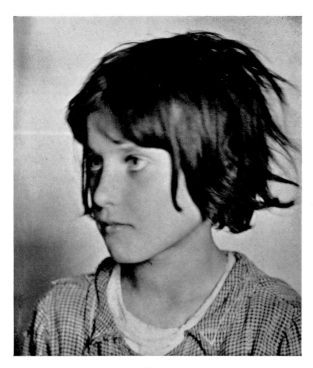

Fig. 3

Fig. 4

For comment on these illustrations and an explanation of their relationship, see p. 22

ART AND COUNTERFEIT

BY

MARGARET H. BULLEY

AUTHOR OF "ANCIENT AND MEDIEVAL ART"

WITH 188 ILLUSTRATIONS

METHUEN & CO. LTD.
36 ESSEX STREET W.C.
LONDON

First Published in 1925

PRINTED IN GREAT BRITAIN

MEMORABILIA

THE arts do not simply imitate the visible thing, but go back to the principle of its nature.   PLOTINUS

In art the terms ancient and modern have no place.   HSIEH HO (6th cent. A.D.)

. . . The truth and nature of things confirmed by the authority of works whose form is not of *one* country or of *one* age.   COLERIDGE

We cannot adequately speak of a high work of art without speaking of art in general.   GOETHE

The true beauties of art are eternal and will be accepted by all ages, but they wear the dress of their century.   DELACROIX

The poet should seize the Particular and he should, if there be anything sound in it, represent the Universal. . . . A man must live from within outwards seeing that, make what contortions he will, he can only bring to light his own individuality.   GOETHE

_____

At bottom it is always this. A man must feel deeply himself before he can rouse feeling in others.   MILLET

Inspiration is the instantaneous solution of a long meditated problem.   NAPOLEON

Fancy abandoned by reason produces impossible monsters : united with it, she is the mother of all the arts and origin of its wonders.   GOYA

In looking at objects of nature . . . I seem to be rather seeking, as if I were *asking* for, a symbolic language for what is within me . . . than observing anything new.   COLERIDGE

Things in respect of themselves have peradventure their weights and measures and conditions : but when we take them into ourselves, the soul forms them as she pleases.   MONTAIGNE

Art is the metaphysical activity of man.   NIETZSCHE

The critic is every instant on the edge of metaphysics.   BAUDELAIRE

The secret of art lies in the artist himself.   KUO JO-HSI (12th cent. A.D.)

It is with . . . all the arts as with children—only those live that have drained much of the author's life into them.   SAMUEL BUTLER

_____

Painting is a craft like carpentry or ironworking : it is subject to the same rules. . . . In following nature one does what one likes and ends, of necessity, in isolation. I remain in the ranks.   RENOIR

Art standeth firmly fixed in nature, and who so can rend her forth, he only possesseth her.   DÜRER

_____

Art is at once the surest escape from the world and the most certain union with it.   GOETHE

Where no arts flourish, where all learning is exterminated, there is no trace of a good man, but cruelty and horrid barbarism stalk abroad.   MILTON

_____

Reflection, from whatever quarry extracted, is the foundation of solid pleasures, which foundation, we think, cannot be laid too early in the season.   LANDOR

To any vision must be brought an eye adapted to what is to be seen.   PLOTINUS

It is not what the teacher does for the pupil, but what the pupil does for himself that matters.   SOCRATES

v

INTRODUCTION

THIS book is an attempt to supply a general text-book on the nature of art and on artistic appreciation. It is planned for the teacher and critic; for the art student, whose mind should be saturated with the sense of design; for those who furnish houses; for the manufacturer who wishes to raise the artistic level of his productions; for those in authority, who may have made no serious study of art, but are compelled by their positions to choose between true and counterfeit works of art for public collections, or approve plans for building and development in town and country. Lastly, it is written for all those interested in art who wish to further their studies at home and abroad.

To some, parts of the book may seem too elementary; to others, too advanced. But the subject has been treated in its simplest and in its most difficult aspects, not only that the study should be as complete as possible, but also in the hope that all classes of inquirers may find something to give them food for thought.

I have believed for some time that an introduction to the study of art should consist, in the main, of a series of illustrations arranged in a particular way, a way that I have proved, through lecturing, to be useful; and that the text accompanying the illustrations should represent the points of view of good critics of many ages and countries rather than the opinions of any single writer.[1] In this book I have assembled such material.

The commentary that follows each series of quotations has been added to bring the quotations and illustrations into a more direct relationship. It is hoped that it will be of service to those who find themselves in need of further guidance. The specialist can ignore it and use the quotations and illustrations to check his own theory. Anyone who wishes can restate the theory of this book in terms of psychology or philosophy, or adapt or adopt any part of it in accordance with a personal æsthetic. Or he may reject the whole and build afresh with the help of the illustrations alone. The book may be regarded as a quarry. To assist independent inquiry, and enable unbiased judgments to be registered first, names and periods have not been printed under the illustrations. They are to be found in the Appendix at the end of the book.

It is to be remembered that though the written word may be suggestive, stimulating, and useful as a signpost to prevent the following of wrong paths and to point the way to

[1] No attempt has been made to include the points of view of the modern psychologist or biologist, as the book is not a psychological or scientific treatise.

right experience, it is only by such experience, personally felt, that the nature of art can be realised. For this reason the illustrations are far the most important part of the book.[1] Understanding grows by making comparisons. Consciously or unconsciously we learn to discriminate between true and counterfeit works of art by comparing one thing with another, or by referring what is before us to the memories of other things we have seen. If we have sensibility, the good things will eventually drive out the bad.

The power to enjoy art is possessed by most people, and awaits cultivation. But under modern conditions such an understanding can only be a slow growth. Some people are born with unusual aptitude, but for most of us it is a case of training what faculty we may possess by long study of genuine works of art of all kinds, all countries, and all ages. In considering the comparisons given in this book we may privately echo the remark of a boy who said : " It is quite easy to choose. All that I think ugly I say are art, and all that I think beautiful I say are not art." Or we may agree with a small girl who was heard to sigh, when a number of sentimental paintings passed before her on the screen : " Not art, but how lovely ! " If so, let us be equally honest, and not pretend to an admiration we do not feel. But, on the other hand, it is worth while to be patient. If we look long at these comparisons, and repeatedly return to them, we may, in time, find that the works of art which seemed at first strange, ugly, or even ridiculous, are now beginning to wear a different aspect. Something in our minds is changing. Perhaps after all . . . ? Even the games-captain of a public school has been known to send a message through his headmaster begging for a third lecture on " goods and bads," because he was just beginning to understand the difference between them.

Although in some instances a minor work of art may be contrasted with a master-piece, many of the reproductions compared at the end of the book represent as sharp a contrast as could be found in order that the difference should be driven home to those who are studying the subject for the first time. The difficulty of our day is that we are surrounded by ugly things, and it is natural for us to like what is familiar and mistrust unaccustomed reactions. It is probable that painting and sculpture have at all times been admired, not so much for their formal qualities, as for their illustrative and technical interests, and their power to stimulate the emotions. We may think we are interested in art but in reality we are interested in description or history, archæology or craft, excellent things in themselves but something other than the matter in hand, for they can be found equally in counterfeit works of art.[2] Unfortunately it is also true that many people patronise art for purposes of social advancement and self-advertisement.

---

[1] Most of the illustrations are of paintings and sculpture because these are the hardest forms of art to understand. It is to be remembered that the study of illustrations can never take the place of the study of actual works of art.

[2] Appreciation of art may, of course, be subconscious. We may enjoy the artistic qualities of an object, and be affected by them, but because this enjoyment has not become articulate we may replace our object by one in-

For convenience the word " art " has been used throughout in its narrower and generally accepted sense instead of the more exact but unwieldy term " visual arts " : also in one or two instances the quotations refer to the arts of poetry and music. In all such cases the passages cited will be found applicable to the visual arts also. The painter, sculptor, or architect is not usually fluent in any medium but that of his own craft, while the poet, using his own language, relates his experience to his own art, although the application may well be used more widely. It will also be found that different writers attach different meanings to certain words, for example, " æsthetic," " intellect," " composition," " decoration," " symbol," etc. Such diversities are inevitable when passages from the writings of many schools of thought, and many ages, are grouped together. But no contradiction should be found in the general trend of the ideas expressed.

It must be clearly understood that this book makes no attempt to deal adequately with æsthetics in general or with the nature of a work of art as a whole, but is occupied, in the main, with one element in a work of art, namely design, and with the reaction to design in taste and appreciation. Even as regards design the problem of its origin has scarcely been mentioned, while the equally important question of its relationship to tools, materials and craft is only touched upon. There is little or no discussion of such matters as the subjective or objective character of art ;[1] the nature of beauty in all its manifestations ; the activities of the conscious and subconscious mind in artistic creation and appreciation ; the expression in art of the artist's personality and mood ; the relationship of the artist to his age and country ; the part that tradition plays in art ; and other similar questions.

The List of Quotations in the Appendix will show where a discussion of many of these questions can be found, while Chapter VII contains passages which deal with the relation of art to morality, religion, and the spiritual life. These are questions which present much difficulty to many people who are beginning a study of art. The sanctity of beauty is no longer as easy to understand as the sanctity of goodness and truth.

It may be well to meet in advance two possible objections. The first deals with the question of comparison. It may be objected that things which are different cannot be compared, and that only similarities are comparable. To this it can be answered that any element in any given whole may be compared and that a " parity of principle " may be looked for. For example, no two individuals can truly be compared, but we can find if

ferior, without realising that something valuable has been lost and a different form of interest or pleasure substituted. But this state of affairs cannot be as common as a complete indifference to art. When right unconscious preferences are reinforced by reflection, good taste should become more firmly entrenched and less subject to disturbance by passing fashion or wrong suggestion. The whole mind will be united in the interest and delight to be found in art.

[1] The trend of modern philosophic and psychological criticism is to describe a work of art as an attitude of mind and to define line, mass, space, design, etc., in terms of experience. In this book this extremely difficult aspect of art will not be discussed, and the elements of a work of art mentioned above will be treated as the qualities of objects. The main purpose of this book is practical, and a discussion of the objective or subjective character of art would do nothing to help the development of good taste.

each has sincerity, courage, unselfishness, or insincerity, cowardice, selfishness. And we can roughly group people as fine, or less fine. But we cannot *grade* fine people. Each is fine in his own fashion. In the same way we can recognise the presence or absence in painting, sculpture, building, and the applied arts of the peculiar virtues of art, but we cannot say that a masterpiece by Giotto or Piero della Francesca is greater than a masterpiece by Titian or Rembrandt, or that a Greek temple is greater than a mediæval church. We cannot say that Fig. 84 is more beautiful than Fig. 79. Each work achieves beauty on its own level. But we can say that the former is greater than the latter.

The second criticism might urge that too much occupation with the analysis of art might tend to make people so rational in their approach to works of art as to be incapable of imaginative and spontaneous understanding. I can only say that this has not been my experience. There is no reason to think that an analytic study of art, rightly conducted, hampers that life of the imagination which art demands for its understanding. To those without imagination art will always remain a closed book. But to-day, as we have said, works of art arouse in too many minds only the interests of subject-matter, technique, archæology, or the sense of the past. The secondary importance of such considerations is exposed by analytic study, and the mind freed to lose itself in the peculiar experience that art provides.

Living with works of art does not necessarily result in appreciation of art. This must have struck anyone sensitive to art who has seen many of the great town and country houses at home and abroad. Only too often will their present owners introduce portraits or furniture or decorations which are an insult to their companions of an older and wiser tradition. And how often has life in a beautiful university matured the taste of the undergraduate? Modern conditions of life have almost destroyed the living tradition of design which was once our heritage, and what we have lost unconsciously must be regained by any means available.

It must not be inferred from the title of this book that a precise line can be drawn between true, and false or counterfeit works of art. Between the genuine works that have stood the test of time and the ebb and flow of fashion, and the mass of merely illustrative and commercial products that competent critics would condemn, lie countless works of varying degrees of merit about which critical opinion will differ. By this I do not refer merely to contemporary art, upon which time will deliver judgment, but to that great mass of work which is neither very good nor very bad. In such work we are conscious of the authentic impulse of art struggling with the impulses that tend to destroy formal unity and equilibrium. When complete harmony has not been achieved, when this unity and equilibrium have not been adequately felt and expressed in design, our pleasure in the work will always be incomplete, although many of its elements may delight us. Perhaps few works of art are perfect, particularly when complex experiences are involved. Many a great artist, on his death-bed, has deplored the cutting-off of his powers at a moment when he felt he was still only on the threshold of mastery of his art. In regard to works of uncertain merit each must judge for himself. Each must affix his label of *true* or *counterfeit* in accordance with his personal recognition of the ascendancy in any work of the powers that make for life, or of those that make for dissolution and oblivion.[1]

In regard to the quotations, if any living writer should feel misrepresented by my severance of a part of his writings from its context, I offer him sincere apologies. The list of quotations will show the reader where he can find the full exposition of any point of view that has interested him. With reference to the arrangement of the material, a certain amount of repetition has been inevitable as each chapter deals largely with the same subject-matter. But a different aspect of the subject has been emphasised in each section, and perhaps there may be advantages in this varied approach to the central theme. Repetition also occurs among the passages quoted, but it should be interesting and illuminating to see different minds of different ages and countries, attacking the same problems and arriving, in spite of minor contradictions, at the same conclusions in regard to the points at issue. No attempt has been made to illustrate the quotations with works of art which the writers might themselves have chosen. I have made the applications that seemed best to me, and in one instance (Fig. 81) have presented as counterfeit art a water-colour by a painter whom Ruskin highly praised.

In conclusion, may I repeat three points that seem to me important?

1. If, after a first study of this book, a new-comer to the subject finds himself able to discriminate between the true and counterfeit works presented, will he remember that art is a profound and difficult subject? The perception of a theory may not imply its comprehension. Except in people of unusual sensibility, an understanding of design and the experience that design communicates can only come with years of familiarity with great art of all kinds.[2]

2. Even the most sensitive person, in laying down this book, will be unable to put in words all that he means by the term " design." He will still be unable to prove the presence of design in beautiful works, or its absence in counterfeits. The complete experience eludes translation into the medium of words. But among people of sensibility a common experience will be recognised although, even here, differences will arise between individuals in regard to particular works. No taste is infallible. A work of art embodies many interests besides the artistic : prejudice, temperament, habit of mind, and wrong suggestion may obscure the recognition of artistic value, or ascribe it to counterfeit works of art. It is difficult and perhaps impossible for one person to share completely the experience of another. Time alone will separate the wise critics from the unwise,

---

[1] It may be objected that the terms " good art " and " bad art " should be substituted for " true art " and " false " or " counterfeit " art. Here again a discussion of such a question would be out of place. The purpose of the book is practical, and critics who share a common experience will understand each other's classifications whatever names they bear.

[2] See Appendix for a report of a test in artistic appreciation.

ignoring the ebb and flow of fashion, and correcting the reactions of each generation against the enthusiasms of its predecessor.

3. Lastly, let the reader have much patience ! If, after reading part of this book, he is tempted to throw it down in despair of comprehending what is meant by " design," let him read to the end, and, still more, make many and long references to the illustrations. The time has come when a scientific age demands that its instinctive experience should be backed by reason. But the subject of art, as already stated, is not easy to present, even partially, in words.

Since the beauty of art lies in design, two sentences from one of Goethe's imaginary conversations can well bring this introduction to a close :

" Can you tell me what beauty is ? "

" Perhaps not, but I can show it to you."

M. H. B.

September 1925

CONTENTS

(For Plates see end of book)

ACKNOWLEDGMENTS

I WISH to express my thanks to Mr. J. Hope-Johnstone, Mr. R. R. Tatlock, and Mr. W. G. Constable for valuable advice, criticism, or expressions of opinion, either given in connection with this book, or garnered during the course of many discussions on the nature of art ; also to Mr. D. Gourlay, for his help in obtaining photographs ; and to my mother for reading the proofs.

I also wish to thank all those authors and publishers of modern works who so kindly gave me permission to reproduce passages from their works and also all other publishers to whom I am indebted for extracts from older books. The names of all these authors and publishers will be found in the Appendix at the end of the book.

I have pleasure in thanking the directors and owners of national and private collections who generously furnished me with photographs or gave me leave to reproduce objects from their collections ; also those authors, editors, and publishers who allowed me to reproduce illustrations from their articles and books, and those teachers of art who lent me work by their pupils for reproduction. Their names, or the names of the collections which they control, will be found in the Appendix.

I am also indebted to the editor of *The Burlington Magazine* for permission to reprint a leading article, a report on a test in artistic appreciation, and certain of the illustrations and quotations in this book which first appeared in their present connection in *The Burlington Magazine* ; to Mr. J. Hope-Johnstone for his kindness in taking two photographs for this book ; to Mr. Laurence Binyon for lending me his reproduction of the landscape by Ma Yuan ; and to Sir Robert and Lady Witt for the frequent use that I have made of their library.

In conclusion I would like to add that I am alone responsible for the opinions expressed in the arguments and commentaries of this book, and for the choice and arrangement of the quotations and illustrations.

M. H. B.

September 1925

ART AND COUNTERFEIT

CHAPTER I

ART AND IMITATION

ARGUMENT.—Art does not necessarily imply imitation of nature. The forms of nature result from, and are controlled by, natural law. The forms of art draw their vitality from, and are controlled by, the life of the mind. The artist who merely copies the appearances of objects and scenes has failed to communicate any experience of reality he may have had.

(I)

AGENT (of an artist) : And do you not at the opera experience a complete deception ?

SPECTATOR : Deception ? that is not the proper word—and yet, yes ! But no. . . .

AGENT : The feeling you have at the exhibition of an opera cannot be rightly called deception ?

SPECTATOR : I agree. Still it is a sort of deception ; something nearly allied to it.

AGENT : Tell me, do you not almost forget yourself . . . namely, when all is harmony. . . . Did this complete representation harmonise with itself or some other natural product ?

SPECTATOR : With itself, certainly.

AGENT : And this harmony was a work of art ?

SPECTATOR : It must have been.

AGENT : We have denied to the opera a certain sort of truth. We have maintained that it is by no means faithful to what it professes to represent. But can we deny to it a certain interior truth, which arises from its completeness as a work of art ?

SPECTATOR : When the opera is good, it creates a little world of its own, in which all proceeds according to fixed laws, which must be judged by its own laws, felt according to its own spirit.

AGENT : Does it not follow from this, that truth of nature and truth of art are two different things, and that the artist neither should nor may endeavour to give his work the air of a work of nature ?

SPECTATOR : But yet it has so often the air of a work of nature.

AGENT : That I cannot deny. But may I on the other hand be equally frank ?

SPECTATOR : Why not ? Our business is not now with compliments.

AGENT : I will then venture to affirm that a work of art can seem only to be a work of nature to a wholly uncultivated spectator ; such a one the artist appreciates and values indeed, though he stands on a lower step. But, unfortunately, he can only be satisfied when the artist descends to his level ; he will never rise with him, when prompted by his genius, the true artist must take wing in order to complete the whole circle of his work.

SPECTATOR : You say that a work of art could appear as a work of nature only to an uncultivated person ?

AGENT : Certainly. You remember the birds that tried to eat the cherries of the great master ?

SPECTATOR : Now, does that not show that the cherries were admirably painted ?

AGENT : By no means. It rather convinces me that these connoisseurs were true sparrows.

SPECTATOR : I cannot, however, for this reason concede that this work could have been other than excellent.

AGENT : Shall I tell you a more modern story ?

SPECTATOR : I would rather listen to stories than to arguments.

AGENT : A certain great naturalist, among other domesticated animals, possessed an ape, which he missed one day, and found after a long search, in his library. There sat the beast on the ground with the plates of an unbound Natural History scattered about him . . . the dainty ape had been making his dinner of the beetles that were pictured in various places.

SPECTATOR : It is a droll story.

AGENT : And seasonable, I hope. You would not compare these coloured copper plates with the work of so great an artist ?

SPECTATOR : No, indeed.

AGENT : But you would reckon the ape among the uncultivated amateurs ?

SPECTATOR : Yes, and among the greedy ones ! You awaken in me a singular idea. Does not the uncultivated amateur, just in the same way, desire a work to be natural, that he may be able to enjoy it in a natural, which is often a vulgar and common way ?

AGENT : I am entirely of that opinion.

SPECTATOR : And you maintain, therefore, that an artist lowers himself when he has to produce this effect ?

AGENT : Such is my firm conviction. . . . The true connoisseur feels that he must collect himself out of his scattered life, must live with the work of art, see it again and again, and through it receive a higher existence.   GOETHE

(2)

Equally little can imitation, realism, serve, as many people think, as a measure of this quality of art. Imitation cannot be such a measure, for the chief characteristic of art is the infection of others with a feeling the artist has experienced, and infection with a feeling is not only not identical with the description of the accessories of what is transmitted, but is usually hindered by superfluous details. The attention of the receiver of the artistic impression is diverted by all these well-observed details, and they hinder the transmission of feeling even when it exists.

To value a work of art by the degree of its realism, by the accuracy of the details, is as strange as to judge of the nutritive quality of food by its external appearance. When we appraise a work according to its realism, we only show that we are talking, not of a work of art, but of its counterfeit. TOLSTOY

(3)

The general belief, in matters of painting and statuary, is this : " I believe in nature, and in nature alone. . . . I believe that art is, and only can be, the reproduction of nature (one timid and dissenting sect wishes that repugnant objects of nature should be excepted). Therefore an industry that gives us results identical with nature will be supreme art." An avenging god gave ear to the prayers of this multitude. Daguerre [1] was his messiah. And then they said : " Because photography gives us all the necessary proofs of exactitude (they thought this, the idiots !), art is photography." . . . From this moment strange abominations were produced. . . . I am convinced that the evolution of photography, badly applied, has largely contributed, as all former purely material progress has contributed, to the impoverishment of art. . . . Day by day art began to lose its self-respect, to humble itself, to prostrate itself before external reality, and the painter became more and more inclined to paint, not his dream, but what he saw. . . . Will the common-sense observer affirm that the invention of photography and the great folly of industrialism have no connection with this strange result ? Can one possibly believe that a people whose eyes have become used to accepting the results of material science as works of beauty, have not markedly, after a certain time, diminished their faculty of judging and feeling all that is most ethereal and spiritual ?

In recent times we have heard said, in a thousand different ways, " Copy nature, only copy nature. There is no greater delight, no greater triumph, than an excellent copy of nature." And this doctrine, the enemy of art, pretends to be applicable to all arts. . . . It would be philosophic to ask . . . if (these doctrinaires) are quite certain of the existence of external nature, or, should this question be too pointed for them, if they are quite sure that they understand *all nature*, all that is embodied in nature. A " yes " would be the most boastful, the most extravagant, of answers. In so far as I can understand their strange and disgraceful ramblings, the pedants . . . would say : " We have no imagination, and we discredit any one who has."
Mysterious faculty, this queen of faculties ! She is in contact with all others, she excites them, she sends them into battle . . . she is analyst and synthesist . . . she disintegrates all creation, and with the materials which she amasses and arranges according to rules of which the origin can only be found in the depths of the soul, she creates a new world, gives us the feeling of something new. BAUDELAIRE

(4)
All art is great and good and true only in so far as it is distinctively the work of

---

[1] The inventor of the daguerreotype.

manhood in its highest sense—that is to say not the work of limbs and fingers, but of the soul, aided, according to her necessities, by the inferior powers ; and therefore distinguished in essence from all products of those inferior powers unhelped by the soul. For as a photograph is not a work of art, though it requires certain delicate manipulations of paper and acid, and subtle calculations of time, in order to bring out a good result, so neither would a drawing *like* a photograph, made directly from nature, be a work of art, although it would imply many delicate manipulations of the pencil and subtle calculation of effects of colour and shade. It is no more art to manipulate a camel's-hair pencil, than to manipulate a china tray and a vial glass. It is no more art to lay on colour delicately than to lay on acid delicately. It is no more art to use the cornea and retina for the reception of an image than to use a lens and a piece of silvered paper. . . .

. . . I do not mean to speak of the body and soul as separable. The man is made up of both ; they are to be raised and glorified together, and all art is the expression of one by, and through, the other. . . . By work of the soul I mean the reader always to understand the work of the entire immortal creature, proceeding from a quick, perceptive, and eager heart, perfected by the intellect, and finally dealt with by the hands, under the direct guidance of these higher powers.

Now observe, while as it penetrates into the nature of things, the imagination is pre-eminently a beholder of things, *as* they *are*, it is, in its creative function, an eminent beholder of things *when* and *where* they are NOT ; a seer, that is, in the prophetic sense, calling " the things that are not as though they were," and for ever delighting to dwell on that which is not tangibly present. And its great function being the calling forth, or back, that which is not visible to bodily sense, it has, of course, been made to take delight in the fulfilment of its proper function and pre-eminently to enjoy and to spend its energy on things past and future or out of sight. . . .

It follows evidently . . . that a picture has in some measure even an advantage with us in not being real. . . . And thus so far from its being at all an object to the painter to make his work look real, he ought to dread such a consummation as the loss of one of its most precious claims upon the heart. So far from striving to convince the beholder that what he sees is substance, his mind should be to what he paints as the fire to the body on the pile, burning away the ashes, leaving the unconquerable shade—an immortal dream. So certain is this that the slightest local success in giving the deceptive appearance of reality—the imitation, for instance, of the texture of a bit of wood, with its grain in relief—will instantly destroy the charm of the whole picture ; the imagination feels itself insulted and injured, and passes by with cold contempt ; nay, however beautiful the whole scene may be, as of late in much of our highly wrought painting for the stage, the mere fact of its being deceptively real is enough to make us tire of it ; we may be surprised and pleased for a moment, but the imagination will not on those terms be persuaded to give any of its help. . . .

And thus it is, that, for the most part, imperfect sketches, outlines, nude sculptures, and other forms of abstraction, possess a charm which the most finished picture frequently wants.

RUSKIN

(5)

Nature is only a dictionary. . . . Nobody has ever considered a dictionary to be a *composition* in the poetic sense of the word. Painters who obey their imagination hunt in their dictionaries for those elements which suit their conceptions. Then, by the most subtle adjustments, they transfigure them. Those who have no imagination copy the dictionary. A great vice results from this, the vice of banality. . . . By looking and copying, they forget to feel and to think. . . .

The visible world is only a shop full of images and signs to which imagination gives relative value and place. It is a kind of pasture-land which imagination should order and transform. All the faculties of the human soul should be subordinated to the imagination which uses them all simultaneously.   DELACROIX *to* BAUDELAIRE

(6)

Nature contains the elements, in colour and form, of all pictures, as the keyboard contains the notes of all music.

But the artist is born to pick and choose, and group with science, these elements, that the result may be beautiful—as the musician gathers his notes and forms his chords, until he brings forth from chaos glorious harmony.

To say to the painter that Nature is to be taken as she is, is to say to the player that he may sit on the piano.   WHISTLER

(7)

Shall painting be confined to the sordid drudgery of facsimile representations of merely mortal and perishing substances, and not be as poetry and music are, elevated into its own proper sphere of invention and visionary conception ?

No ! it shall not be so ! Painting as well as poetry and music exists and exults in immortal thoughts. . . .

A spirit and a vision are not, as the modern philosophy supposes, a cloudy vapour or a nothing. They are organised and minutely articulated beyond all that the mortal and perishing nature can produce.

He who does not imagine in stronger and better lineaments and in stronger and better light than his perishing mortal eye can see, does not imagine at all. The painter of this work insists that all his imaginations appear to him infinitely more perfect and more minutely organised than anything seen by his mortal eye.

I question not my corporal eye any more than I would question a window concerning a sight. I look through it and not with it.

Men think they can copy nature as correctly as I copy imagination.
                                                        WILLIAM BLAKE

(8)

To paint from nature is to realise one's sensations, not to copy what is before one.
                                                        CÉZANNE *to* VOLLARD

Art is a harmony, parallel with the harmony of nature. What is one to think of the idiots who say to one, " The painter is always inferior to nature." He is parallel with it —unless he deliberately intervenes. You must grasp that clearly. He must silence in himself all prejudiced voices, forget, forget, be a perfect echo. Then the whole landscape will imprint itself upon his sensitive plate. To fix it on the canvas, to externalise it, craft will then intervene, but a respectful craft, also prepared only to obey, to translate unconsciously, because it knows the language so well, the text which it spells out, the two parallel texts—live nature *felt*, that which is there (he indicated the green and blue plain); that which is here (he struck his forehead), so that both of them may fuse in order to endure, to live a life half human, half divine, the life of art, do you see . . . the life of God. The landscape is reflected, is humanised, it realises itself in me. I objectify it, project it, fix it on my canvas. . . . The landscape and my canvas are both of them outside myself, but one chaotic, fugitive, confused, without logical life, existing outside reason : the other permanent, sentient, systematised, taking part in the life of to-day, in the drama of ideas, in their individuality. I have it ! It's an interpretation.

Deep feeling unifies the whole being. The rush of the world at the bottom of the mind resolves itself with the same motion that the eyes, the ears, the mouth, the nose discover, each according to its own lyricism. . . . And art, I believe, puts us in the state of grace when universal emotion reveals itself to us, religiously, yet very naturally. The universal harmony, like colour, should be found everywhere. . . . Every woodland scent I can hear in Weber. In the depths of the verses of Racine I feel a local tone, as of Poussin, just as in certain purples of Rubens lingers an ode, a murmur, a rhythm, as of Ronsard.

Genius creates its own method . . . my own, I have no other, is hatred of the imaginative. I want to be as stupid as a cabbage. My method, my code, is realism. But realism, understand clearly, that is full of grandeur.

All this sunburnt landscape is like an unearthly Eclogue, the universe, balanced for a moment, and held in its most human joy.

In the painter there are two things, the eye and the brain : each should help the other. Both must be developed, but in the fashion of a painter ; the eye by the vision of nature, the brain by the logic of organised sensations, which provide the means of expression. . . . The eye should concentrate, devour ; the brain formulate. . . .
We identify ourselves with objects, we are carried away by them.

CÉZANNE *to* GASQUET

(9)

My sculpture is not copied from nature. . . . I follow a definite and preconceived idea about sculpture, and from that I make a sketch in clay. . . . What I search for is the disposition of volume in space, the figure in light and air. I search for an ample form and the copying of an actual figure is of no interest to me. . . . Who could copy nature ? Even the Greeks never attempted it. . . . What is important is the general idea. It can't be explained, but has to be felt.

Do you want to know my æsthetic ? Well, here it is (he took a pencil and paper and drew an egg). You see, this line goes one way and the other exactly the opposite. Here is a flower. One side like this, the other again exactly the opposite. Nature always proceeds symmetrically with harmonious forms. Every potter knows that instinctively. He makes one side of his pot just like the other. I apply the same principle to the human figure. One side like this, the opposite the same. And then again all perpendicular and vertical lines in nature are straight : all horizontals round. Take a tree-trunk. Its vertical lines are as straight as a candle. Cut it across and all the forms are round. Apply these principles which I have found in nature and you have the basis of my æsthetic. But don't take it too literally. The Cubists, you see, are quite clever and talented people, but with them the letter has killed the spirit. They have read Plato and everything for them is now idea. Believe me, Plato would be horrified at their works, and would prefer the firm breasts of my stone goddesses to their Cubist constructions.

The Cubists say that they want a non-sensuous, decent art. What folly ! Sensuousness is the essence of art. How can it be produced if not by the senses ? And then observe nature. The sea, the sun, wine. . . . Nature is good, and sane, and strong. One must live with her and listen to her voice, and then one may produce fine art. Harmony in nature ? I always try and express it in art. . . . I seek the grand harmony of forms, so that when they are achieved they will take their place in sun and air inevitably, without effort. I try to bring all the parts into harmony. I fit them together always comparing each to the whole. Without copying nature I work like nature. . . . Sculpture must have mass. Nothing is more hideous than meagre figures. Sculpture must make us certain and serene.   MAILLOL

(10)

If the artist copies the mere nature, the *natura naturata*, what idle rivalry ! If he proceeds from a given form, which is supposed to answer to the notion of beauty, what an emptiness, what an unreality there always is in his productions . . . ! Believe me, you must master the essence, the *natura naturans*, which presupposes a bond between nature in the higher sense and the soul of man. . . .

. . . To make the external internal, and the internal external . . . this is the mystery of genius in the fine arts.   COLERIDGE

(11)

In landscape painting there are six essentials—*Spirit, Harmony, Thought, Atmosphere, Brush*, and *Ink*. *Spirit* makes the heart travel with the brush and seize unerringly the shapes of things. *Harmony*, without visible contours, suggests form ; omits nothing yet escapes vulgarity. *Thought* segregates the essential and concentrates the mind on the shapes of things. . . .

The *Marvellous Painter* is profuse in ill-considered forms. Often while achieving resemblance in detail he misses the universal principles of the view before him. This is the result of a mechanical dexterity without intelligence. The *Skilful Painter* scrapes together little prettinesses and welds them into the pretence of a masterpiece, but the more he loads his design with decoration, the further he recedes from the true spirit of the scenes which he depicts. When the operation of the spirit is weak, all the forms are defective; and though the brush be active, its production will be like dead things; then we speak of "faults unconnected with representations."

CHING HAO (10th century)

(12)

Let no one repeat to me again that absurd maxim, "We must have novelty, we must belong to our century; everything changes and is changed." What a sophism! Does nature change, do the light and the air change, have the passions of the human heart changed since Homer? "One must belong to one's own century." But suppose one's century is wrong? Because my neighbour does wrong, am I to do wrong also? Because you misunderstand nature and beauty, must I misunderstand in my turn and imitate you? . . . Homer and Phidias, Raphael and Poussin, Gluck and Mozart, have said, in reality, the same things. . . . There is only one art . . . that which is based on the imitation of nature,[1] on immutable, infallible, eternal beauty. Believe what they have believed, that is to say, the truth, the truth that is for all time. Our translation must differ from theirs in the expression, but we must know, as they knew, how to recognise truth, honour it, in spirit and in principle.

In studying nature, only have eyes at first for the general effects. Consider it, and consider it only. Details are of small importance and must take their proper place. Noble form, and still more noble form! it is the basis and conditioner of the whole. Even smoke should translate itself in this fashion.

Do you think I want to make copyists of you? No, I want you to take the sap from the plant.

INGRES

(13)

There is an absolute necessity for the Painter to generalise his notions; to paint particulars is not to paint Nature, it is only to paint circumstances. When the artist has conceived in his imagination the image of perfect beauty, or the abstract idea of forms, he may be said to be admitted into the great council of Nature.

SIR JOSHUA REYNOLDS

(14)

" I will treat you to something good by way of dessert," said he. With these words he placed before me a landscape by Rubens. . . . "There is something very particular attached to this . . . picture. . . . All these things which we see represented . . . on which side are they lighted? . . . This dark ground . . . whence does it arise?" "It is the powerful shadow," said I, "thrown by the group of trees towards the figure. But how?" I continued with surprise. "The figures cast their shadows into the picture; the group of trees on the contrary, cast theirs towards the spectator. We have, thus, light from two different sides, which is quite contrary to Nature."

"That is the point," returned Goethe with a smile. "It is by this that Rubens proves himself great, and shows to the world that he, with a free spirit, stands *above* Nature, and treats her conformably to his high purposes. The double light is certainly

---

[1] By *imitation*, Ingres does not, of course, mean servile copying. See the two following passages.

a violent expedient, and you truthfully say that it is contrary to Nature. But if it is contrary to Nature I say that it is higher than Nature. I say it is a bold stroke of the master, by which he, in a genial manner, proclaims to the world that art is not entirely subject to natural necessities, but has laws of its own. . . .

" The artist has a twofold relation to Nature, he is at once her master and her slave. He is her slave inasmuch as he must work with earthly things, in order to be understood ; but he is her master inasmuch as he subjects these earthly means to his higher intentions and renders them subservient.

" The artist would speak to the world through an entirety ; however, he does not find this entirety in Nature, but it is the fruit of his own mind, or if you like it, of the aspirations of a fructifying divine breath.

" If we observe this landscape by Rubens only slightly, everything appears as natural to us as if it had been copied exactly from Nature. But this is not the case. So beautiful a picture has never been seen in Nature, any more than a landscape of Poussin or Claude Lorrain, which appear very natural to us but which we vainly seek in the actual world."

GOETHE *to* ECKERMANN

COMMENTARY

A study of the preceding passages makes it clear that the first step towards an understanding of art is the realisation that, broadly speaking, there are two different kinds of beauty, the beauty of nature and the beauty of art, and that they do not enter into competition.[1] It is true that we often find the beauty of nature incorporated into the beauty of art, but when this has occurred the work does not owe its beauty as art to the subject-matter it incorporates. To this point we shall return later. The passages just quoted emphasise the difference between these two kinds of beauty. It is illustrated in an elementary form in Fig. 5. We should not think of saying that the beauty of the trees is greater than the beauty of the clipped hedges and grass borders, or *vice versa*, because we realise that each has its own beauty, and that things so dissimilar cannot be compared. Clipped hedges and grass borders can scarcely be described as art, but in their shaping and in the relationship set up between them we are conscious of the elements of art.

In Figs. 6–15 we have five pairs of different renderings of the same subject-matter. Each pair consists of the mechanical version of a camera and the creative and imaginative version of an artist. Experience of art can never be completely translated into the medium of words, but prolonged contemplation of each pair will gradually make it clear that the work of the artist has a unity, a density of matter, an order, a sense of purpose, and above all a vitality, which are lacking in the photographs. Photography may be a minor art, but its main function is always descriptive, as in the instances shown. But in a genuine work of art we are conscious that every part of it has been brought into a definite rhythmic relationship with every other part, and that a mood or state of mind is thus communicated. Note how the figures in No. 6 are scattered disconnectedly and at random, and contrast those in Fig. 7, where we feel that the position of every one is the result of deliberate intention. See in Fig. 9 how the artist has simplified his subject, reducing it to broad, deep masses of light and shade and delicate modulations of tone. He has rejected all details which would mar the unity and balance of the whole, and has left out those archæological and historical aspects of the scene which have nothing to do with art and only interfere with the purpose of pictorial unity. In Figs. 10 and 11, the contrast between the photograph and the colour print of the same subject is very strongly marked. The artist

[1] In a book such as this, the philosophic question of whether natural beauty can exist save by the shaping and interpretating powers of the mind cannot be discussed. It must also be borne in mind that the beauty of nature takes on, to a certain extent, the beauty of art, in so far as we look at nature with the eye of an artist and disengage the formal significance of what we see.

has used the natural forms in a most arbitrary fashion, and built up a simple and decorative scheme in which the Japanese script plays a part and which is very Eastern in character.[1]

Figs. 12 and 13 contrast a photograph and a rapid oil sketch of the same girl. The animation of the sitter has been captured by the artist and embodied in a structure of vigorously modulated and simplified planes in low tones. In Figs. 14 and 15 we see the gulf that separates a fine painting of still life from a photograph. In the picture all the elements are fused into a richly coloured harmony. Each one is related inevitably to the other, and what was uninteresting as a photograph has become charged with the significance of the highly plastic values of a great artist's vision.

The three portraits of Dumas reproduced on Plate V. provide a further comparison of art, counterfeit art, and photography. Whereas the photograph (Fig. 17) has value as a literal record of the writer's appearance, the vigorous painting by Daumier (?) (Fig. 16) transmits the colossal energy and romantic exuberance of Dumas' personality. This has again been achieved by building up new and plastic forms, more realistic in this instance, and carried further, than are the forms in the portrait sketch in Fig. 13. The lithograph (Fig. 18), in common with the majority of modern portraits, has neither the virtues of photography nor of art. We find neither the accuracy of the one nor the vitality of the other.

Figs. 19–22 show four portrait busts. Are they art? Or are they not? The reader is invited to register his personal judgment and then bring into consideration the following points : Fig. 19 (except for the back of the head and the shoulders) is a portrait bust produced by machine process. The face in Fig. 22 is also, with the exception of the eyes, mechanically produced, as it is a cast from a wax impression taken after death. Since art can never be created by mechanical means it follows that these two portrait busts cannot be works of art. No doubt they record the appearance of their subjects, and so have value as long as we are interested in these men or in the types they represent. Indeed they are far more valuable than the average portrait bust produced by sculptors to-day, who attempt, but fail to achieve, an equally accurate likeness. But neither the mechanical nor the imitative busts are animated by the enduring vitality of art which we find in Figs. 20 and 21. It is a vitality born of the power of the artist to see and feel nature in terms of formal unity and equilibrium. As we look long at the busts we see that these arrangements of forms have a sensitive and rhythmic quality, and express purpose, harmony, and that density of matter and intensity of mood which we felt in studying the other comparisons. These qualities raise the subject-matter to a level of universal significance. We are aware of troubled concentration, power, resolution, rather than of an Italian general of the Renaissance : of reverie, imagination, and sensibility in their essence rather than of the likeness of a dreamy Egyptian king. The lyric quality of the Egyptian bust moves us almost as music moves us. In each case we feel that we are in contact with reality. In such contact it does not matter whether or not we realise that the experience we receive is communicated by the peculiar relationship of planes, a relationship resulting from feeling rather than from thought. We know now something of what Coleridge meant when he spoke of making the external internal and the internal external, and the intentions of the other quotations should be clearer. But we must be aware of the different meanings attached to the words *real, reality, life,* and *life-like* when used in relation to art. When Ruskin says (p. 4) that a picture has an advantage in not being *real,* he uses the word in the meaning of photographic accuracy. But the word can be used in another way. We can say that art alone has *reality* when we contrast it with counterfeit art, or works of pure illustration and description, the authors of which either never had the experience of art to communicate, or have had it only in a limited degree, or have had it and failed to transmit it. In the hands of a great artist the authentic experience of art crystallises into the forms of art freely and without inhibition. The sense of reality conveyed by these forms is not that of a clever imitation of nature. It is a reality that cannot be described in words. Similarly with the word *life,* we can speak of a picture being "lifelike" when we mean that it reflects the life of nature as in a

---

[1] The photograph was taken a good many years after the colour print was made, and it is probable that the trees in the foreground of the print were no longer there when the photograph was taken.

mirror. But the significance of the word is very different when we use it to describe the vitality of art which is born of the artist's experience, and communicated to us by a significant arrangement of forms.

Figs. 23–26 are further examples of the presence or absence of vitality. A short consideration of them will convince us that while the photograph of the wrestlers (Fig. 23) gives us only a reflection of a carefully composed but actual struggle, and Fig. 24 a theatrical and wooden picture of a brawl, Figs. 25 and 26 give us art—struggle, tension, effort, presented as dynamic or static by what may now be summed up in the term *design*.

But before the subject of design can be more fully treated, attention must be called to two points. The first is the way in which the child's drawing and the two famous masterpieces on Plate VIII. illustrate the wise neglect of accurate representation in favour of the more serious claims of design. Fig. 28 shows a mental image, charged with feeling, in which the shadows fall sometimes in one direction, sometimes in another. Yet they are imaginatively right. If they were altered, through loyalty to science, the unity of the conception and the sense of something significant and inevitable would perish. In Fig. 29, for similar reasons, Titian has cast one mass of shadow to the left of his picture, one to the right, and one in the foreground. This disposition of the dark masses is contrary to natural law, but the balance established is an integral part of the pictorial structure. Fig. 27 represents a detail of the Parthenon frieze. Even if allowance be made for the smaller size of horses in the days of Phidias and for certain sculptural conventions, it can only be loyalty to art which accounts for the relative size of riders to horses. In these illustrations we find, although on two very different levels of experience, the self-contained world of art described by Goethe on pp. 1 and 8.

Secondly, we must notice a phenomenon peculiar to artistic vision. An artist may seek to copy as closely as possible some object before him, yet what he achieves may be something very different from an accurate reproduction of that object. An example is given in Plate IX. Nos. 1–11 are " bird-man " carvings made by natives of the Solomon Islands. The islanders believe that when a chief dies his spirit inhabits the body of a frigate-bird, and for this reason the bird has a sacred significance for them. Bird and chief are frequently associated in carvings, and gradually a composite bird-man image has developed. Nos. 12 and 13 are sketches of one native by another, one made at the instigation of a European. It will be seen that whereas the native, no doubt, thought he was accurately representing his sitter, he was really reproducing the bird-man image in a fresh guise. In the same way, and in all ages, renderings which have seemed to their authors purely realistic have often been, and in one sense have always been, projections of mental images of which the conscious mind has been unaware.

The differing types of artistic vision can broadly be classed as realistic and non-realistic. Great art can spring from either. But it must be understood that realistic vision in art is never photographic. Facts will be recorded, but they will be so unified and ordered that complete formal significance will be established. Examples of this type of vision are given in Figs. 33 and 34. Here the spectator is not disturbed by those closely observed details of which so many critics speak, because these details have become elements in larger wholes, and are now the servants of an idea, not ends in themselves. Neither the drawing nor the painting could be mistaken for a photograph. The facts of life have suffered a change, and taken on the ideal qualities of form. The solidity and recession of the planes can be felt.

Figs. 31 and 32 are examples of non-realistic vision. The artists have materialised mental images which have but little counterpart in life, although in Fig. 31 it is not difficult to imagine the scene which gave rise to the picture. The tiger in Fig. 32 is a fantastic apparition, never seen but by the eye of the mind. In some of the greatest works of art the objective and subjective elements are so perfectly balanced and harmonised that neither predominates. As examples, Figs. 84 and 142 can be cited.

These preliminary considerations have cleared the approach to the subject of design. The sections that follow will summarise and amplify what has already been said. The illustrations in the present section should be reconsidered after studying the subject-matter of the sections that follow.

CHAPTER II

DESIGN

ARGUMENT.—Art does, of necessity, imply " design " or " form." In all ages of reflection, attempts have been made to define the nature of art. Men have tried to use words, as symbols, to describe what is essentially a spiritual experience ; to explain a harmony and equilibrium that is not completely reasoned, but " felt in the blood and felt along the heart " ; to account for a formal unity and order which have significance as the completion and expression of an idea, the embodiment and communication of a state of mind, rather than as a mere description of facts or an attempt to produce a purely useful article. We feel that in works of art the forms have been fused by some inner heat, and have cooled and set under the direction of higher mental processes, so that we are in contact with reality, with creative energy, with life itself, while at the same time we are at peace. But we realise that reason cannot penetrate to the heart of the experience. This can only be reached imaginatively, through contemplation. Design cannot be taught although in ages of civilisation the critical faculties supplement the intuitive activities and the whole mind unites in the creation of the work of art.

(15)

He will watch from dawn to gloom
The lake-reflected sun illume
The yellow bees in the ivy-bloom,
Nor heed nor see what things they be ;
But from these create he can
Forms more real than living man
Nurselings of immortality.

SHELLEY

(16)

Living form, that is eternal existence.

WILLIAM BLAKE

(17)

I have made use of the word *design* in this essay to express the supreme inventive art of the painter, sculptor, or architect abstractly considered. . . . The great organ or instrument of this art is draught, or drawing. . . .

Drawing is mechanical, and may therefore be taught, in some means, to any person of moderate talents who applies sufficiently to the practice of it ; but design is the child of genius, and cannot be wholly infused. The principle of it must exist in the soul, and can be called forth only by education and improved by practice. Thus the art of numbers may be attained by the ear; the knowledge of bodies, properties, facts, events, and fables by reading. But the *vis poetica*, which distinguishes the bard from the journalist or versifyer, must be the gift of heaven.

Neither the poetic energy nor the inventive power of the designer can be taught in schools or academies; but they both may be buried in rust and inaction, unknown even to professors, if schools and academies do not present the objects that excite and attract them into motion. . . .

The painter, the sculptor, the architect . . . have so near an affinity with the poet, the philosopher, the orator, and the geometrician that there needs no apology for the frequent parallel I have made between them in this essay.   J. GWYN (1749)

(18)

Seeing that design, the parent of our three arts, architecture, sculpture, and painting, having its origin in the intellect, draws out from many single things a general judgment—so that there is formed in the mind that something which afterwards, when expressed by the hands, is called design—we may conclude that design is not other than a visible expression and declaration of our inner conception, and of that which others have imagined and given form to, in their idea. . . .

All these lines and works and ingenious arts, as one sees, are derived from design, which is the necessary fount of all, for, if they are lacking in design, they have nothing.
                                                    GEORGIO VASARI (1511–74)

(19)

Design—that faculty which creates from the pictorial elements it uses an organic unity, holding the parts in equilibrium. . . . Through this balance of organic unity even the stormiest and most violent forms can be held as in a charmed repose. . . . It is the miraculous faculty of design, that without recourse to symbol it can take the simplest of living things and convert them from fact into idea, so that we no longer see merely the object represented, but are somehow admitted with seeing eyes into the mystery of life itself, the something sacred at the heart of things which appeals to what is profoundest in ourselves. Something in us of which we were not conscious, far below the surface of our intelligence, comes up into the light.   LAURENCE BINYON

(20)

(Beauty is a primeval phenomenon which itself never makes its appearance, but the reflection of which is visible in a thousand different utterances of the creative mind, and is as various as Nature herself.   GOETHE)

(21)

Design is the first element, the groundwork, the foundation of all art. . . .
                                                            C. J. HOLMES

(22)

. . . In order therefore to be as brief as possible, I shall define beauty to be a harmony of all the parts in whatsoever subject it appears, fitted with such proportion and connection that nothing could be added, diminished, or altered but for the worse.

. . . Variety is without dispute a very great beauty in everything when it joins and brings together, in a regular manner, things different but proportionate to each other . . . as in music when the base answers the treble and the tenor agrees with both, there arises from that variety of sounds a harmonious and wonderful union of proportions which delights and enchants our senses.

. . . Whatever that property be which is so gathered and collected from the whole number and nature of the separate parts, or to be imparted to each of them according to a certain and regular order, . . . it is certain such a property must have in itself something of the force and spirit of all the parts with which it is either united or mixed, otherwise they must jar and disagree and, by such a discord, destroy the uniformity or beauty of the whole. . . .

The business and office of congruity is to put together members differing from each other in their natures in such a manner that they may conspire to form a beautiful whole. So that when such a composition offers itself to the mind, either by the conveyance of the sight, hearing, or any of the other senses, we immediately perceive this congruity. . . . Nor does this congruity arise so much from the body in which it is found, or any of its members, as from itself, and from nature, so is its true seat in the mind and in reason.

LEONE BAPTISTA ALBERTI (1404–1472)

(23)

Now invention in art signifies an arrangement in which everything in the work is thus consistent with all things else, and helpful to all else. . . . The power by which it is effected is absolutely inexplicable and uncommunicable ; but exercised with entire faculty by those who possess it, in many cases even unconsciously.[1]

In work which is not composed, there may be many beautiful things, but they do not help each other. They at the best only stand beside, and more usually compete with, and destroy, each other. They may be connected artificially in many ways, but the test of their being no invention is that if one of them be taken away, the others are no worse than before. But in true composition, if one be taken away, all the rest are helpless and valueless. Generally, in falsely composed work, if anything be taken away, the rest will look better ; because the attention is less distracted. Hence the pleasure of inferior artists in sketching, and their inability to finish : all that they add destroys.

Also in true composition everything not only helps everything else a *little*, but helps

[1] By diligent study of good compositions it is possible to put work together, so that all the parts shall help each other a little, or at all events do no harm ; and when some tact, or taste, are associated with this diligence, semblances of real inventions are often produced, which, being the results of great labour, the artist is always proud of ; and which, being capable of learned explanation and imitation, the spectator naturally takes interest in. The common precepts about composition all produce and teach this false kind, which, as true composition is the noblest, being the corruption of it, is the ignoblest condition of art.

with its utmost power.   Every atom is full of energy ; and *all* that energy is kind.   Not a line, not a spark of colour, but is doing its very best, and that best is aid.   The extent to which this law is carried in truly right and noble work is wholly unconceivable to the ordinary observer, and no true account of it would be believed.

True composition being entirely easy to the man who can compose, he is seldom proud of it, though he clearly recognises it.   Also true composition is inexplicable.   No one can explain how the notes of a Mozart melody, of the folds of a piece of Titian's drapery, produce their essential effects upon each other.   If you do not feel it, no one can by reasoning make you feel it.   And the highest composition is so subtle it is apt to become unpopular. . . .

The reader may be surprised at my giving so high a place to invention.   But if he ever come to know true invention from false, he will find out not only that it is the highest quality of art, but is simply the most wonderful act or power of humanity.   It is pre-eminently the deed of human creation ; ποίησις, otherwise poetry . . . the suggestion by the imagination of noble grounds for noble emotion.

What . . . is the ruling character of the person who produces . . . the creator or maker anciently called the poet ? . . . You certainly do not talk of creating a watch or creating a shoe ; nevertheless you *do* talk of creating a feeling.   Why is this ?

. . . To create anything in reality is to put life into it.

A poet or creator is therefore a person who puts things together not as a watchmaker steel, or a shoemaker leather, but who puts life into them.

His work is essentially this : it is the gathering and arranging of material by imagination so as to have in it at last the harmony and helpfulness of life and the passion and emotion of life.   Mere fitting and adjustment of material is nothing ; that is watchmaking.   But helpful and passionate harmony . . . is the harmony of Apollo and the Muses.

. . . Such, then, are a few of the great principles by the enforcement of which you may hope to promote the success of the modern student of design ; but, remember, none of these principles will be useful at all, unless you understand them to be, in one profound and stern sense, useless.   That is to say, unless you feel neither you, nor I, nor anyone can, in the great ultimate sense, teach anybody how to make a good design.

If designing *could* be taught, all the world would learn ; as all the world reads or calculates.   But designing is not to be spelled nor summed. . . . Alas ! I could as soon tell you how to make or manufacture an ear of wheat as to make a good artist of any kind. I can analyse the wheat very learnedly for you and tell you there is starch in it, and carbon and silex.   I can give you starch and charcoal and flint ; but you are as far from the ear of wheat as you were before.   All that can possibly be done for anyone who wants ears of wheat is to show them where to find grains of wheat, and how to sow them, and then with patience, in heaven's time, the ears will come—or perhaps will come—ground and weather permitting.   So in this matter of making artists—first you must find your artist, in the grain, then you must plant him ; fence and weed the field about him ; and with patience, ground and weather permitting, you may get an artist out of him—not otherwise.

(The great artist's) method of observation and abstraction are essential habits of his thought, conditions of his being. . . . Titian and Veronese compose as tranquilly as they would speak—inevitably. The thing comes to them so. They see it so—rightly and in harmony: they will not talk to you of composition, hardly even understanding how lower people see things otherwise.

Thus we may reason wisely over the way a bee builds its comb, and be profited by finding out certain things about the angles of it. But the bee knows nothing of these matters. It builds its comb in a far more inevitable way, and from a bee to Paul Veronese, all the master-workers work with this awful, this inspired unconsciousness.

RUSKIN

(24)

One cannot repeat too often that the rules of beauty are eternal and unchangeable, and that its forms are variable. . . .

There is a special emotion which is peculiar to painting. Nothing (in literature) gives an idea of it. It is an impression which results from a certain arrangement of colours, lights, and shadows, etc. It is what one describes as the music of the picture. . . .

The most careful execution of details will not give this unity which springs from some unknown creative power, the source of which is indefinable.

The first strokes by which a clever master expresses his thought hold the germ of all that the work can offer in the way of inspiration. Raphael, Rembrandt, Poussin—I specially mention these because their ideas have been unusually brilliant—dash a few strokes on paper. Every one of them appears inevitable. To intelligent eyes the drawing is already alive in every part.[1]

The first idea, the sketch, which is in a certain sense the egg, or embryo, of the idea, is usually far from being complete; it can, if necessary, embody the essential, but this essential must be disentangled, for it is neither more nor less than the reunion of every part. What makes the sketch the direct expression of the idea is not the suppression of details, but their complete subordination to the main design which should move us before everything else. The greatest difficulty, therefore, consists in subordinating everything in the picture to this effacement of details, although these details are the ingredients, the warp, in fact, of the picture.

I may be mistaken, but I believe that even the greatest artists have had to fight hard against this greatest of all difficulties. From it, rather than from anything else, arises the disadvantage of endowing details with such charm and delicacy of execution that one hates to sacrifice this interest later on when it damages the general effect. It is in this connection that those gifted with an easy and delicate touch, the producers of expressive heads and torsos, find their confusion and their triumph. The picture made up of patch-

[1] See Fig. 42 for drawing by Poussin.

work, skilfully executed and put together, appears to be a masterpiece, the very sum of dexterity, in so far as it is not finished, or, in other words, if the entire surface has not been covered. For to these painters who complete every detail in turn, to have finished is to have covered the canvas. Before this apparently effortless work, before these scraps which interest us so that we cannot help being delighted by them, we are filled with ill-considered astonishment; but when the last touch is given, when the architect of this scrap-heap has completed his motley edifice and said his last word, one sees nothing but gaps and excrescences, without a single trace of order. The interest that has been roused by each part is lost in the confusion; that which seemed perfectly correct in execution becomes aridity itself, owing to the general absence of *sacrifices*. From this largely haphazard reunion of parts, without inevitable connections, how can you possibly expect the direct penetrating impression, the primitive sketch of an idea that the artist feels he has caught a glimpse of and captured, in the first moment of inspiration? With great artists this sketch is not a dream, a cloudy haze; it is something other than a union of hardly realised strokes: great artists alone start from a fixed point, and they can only return to this pure expression with difficulty in the lengthy or rapid execution of their work. How is the mediocre artist to hope to recover it, by means of his craft, when he is absorbed in his astonishing details which disperse, rather than illumine, the idea? It is amazing to what extent the first elements of composition are confused in the minds of a great number of artists. How can they hope to recover, by skill of execution, this idea which they have never had?

. . . A mediocre artist . . . can only invent timidly and copy servilely. . . . If he can infuse a certain amount of interest or even charm into his work, as a result of any personal inspiration with which he may have been endowed, I can only compare his compilation with life as it actually is, with that mixture of delights and mortifications of which it is compounded. DELACROIX

(25)

The safest definition, then, of Beauty, as well as the oldest, is that of Pythagoras: THE REDUCTION OF MANY TO ONE. . . .

The sense of beauty subsists in simultaneous intuitive of the relation of parts, each to each, and of all to a whole; exciting an immediate and absolute complacency without inter-venence therefore, of any interest, sensual or intellectual. . . .

The mystics meant the same when they define beauty as the subjection of matter to spirit, so as to be transformed into a symbol in and through which the spirit reveals itself, and declare *that* the *most* beautiful where the most obstacles to a full manifestation have been most perfectly overcome. I would that . . . readers had Raphael's " Galatea " or his " School of Athens " before them ![1] COLERIDGE

(26)

" You now stand at that point where you must break through to the really high and difficult part of art; the representation of what is individual. . . . The apprehension and representation of the individual is the very life of art. Besides, while you content

---

[1] See Fig. 92 for Raphael's " Disputa," which shows similar characteristics.

2

yourself with generalities every one can imitate you ; but, in this particular, no one can —and why ? Because no others have experienced exactly the same thing.

" And you need not fear lest what is peculiar should not meet with sympathy. Each character, each object which you can represent from the stone up to man, has generality, and there is nothing to be found only once in the world.

" And this step of representing what is individual," continued Goethe, " leads, at the same time, to what we call composition."

This was not at once clear to me, though I refrained from questions. " Perhaps," thought I, " he means the blending of the Ideal with the Real—the union of that which is external with that which is innate. But perhaps he meant something else."

GOETHE to ECKERMANN

(27)

The three kinds of art (music, visual arts, and poetry) . . . always become . . . similar *in their action upon the mind*. . . .

Consummate style in every art manifests itself in knowing how to remove its specific limits, without also abolishing its specific advantages, while a skilful improvement of its peculiarity bestows upon it a more universal character.

And the artist must not only overcome by his treatment the limits which the specific character of his kind of art brings with it, but also those which belong to the particular material which he elaborates. In a genuine work of art the subject should effect nothing, but the form everything ; since the entirety of man is acted upon by form alone, but only single powers by the subject. However noble and comprehensive, then, the subject may be, it is always confined in its influence upon the spirit, and true æsthetic freedom is to be expected only from form. Herein consists the art-secret of the master, *that by the form he abolishes the subject*.

SCHILLER

(28)

Now in what way, we ask, can form in painting give me a sensation of pleasure which differs from the ordinary sensations I receive from form ? How is it that an object whose recognition in nature may have given me no pleasure becomes, when recognised in a picture, a source of æsthetic enjoyment, or that recognition pleasurable in nature becomes an enhanced pleasure the moment it is transferred to art ? The answer, I believe, depends upon the fact that art stimulates to an unwonted activity psychical processes which are in themselves the source of most (if not all) of our pleasures, and which here, free from disturbing physical sensations, never pass over into pain. For instance : I am in the habit of realising a given object with an intensity which we shall value as 2. If I suddenly realise this familiar object with an intensity of 4, I receive the immediate pleasure which accompanies a doubling of my mental activity. But the pleasure rarely stops here. Those who are capable of receiving direct pleasure from a work of art are generally led on to the further pleasures of self-consciousness. The fact that the psychical process of recognition goes forward with the unusual intensity of 4 to 2 overwhelms them with the sense of having twice the capacity they had credited themselves with ; their whole personality is enhanced, and being aware that this enhancement is connected with the object in question, they for some time after take not only an increased interest in it, but continue to realise it with a new intensity.   Precisely this is what form does in paint-ing : it lends a higher coefficient of reality to the object represented, with the consequent enjoyment of accelerated psychical processes, and the exhilarating sense of increased capacity in the observer.[1] . . .

And it happens thus.   We remember that to realise form we must give tactile values to retinal sensations.[2] . . .   Obviously the artist who gives us these values more rapidly than the object itself gives them, gives us the pleasures consequent upon a more vivid realisation of the object, and the further pleasures that come from the sense of greater psychical capacity. . . .

Now, this sense, though it will increase as the man is revealed to himself, is something which the great painter possesses at the start, so that he is scarcely, if at all, aware of possessing it.   His conscious effort is given to the means of rendering.   It is of means of rendering, therefore, that he talks to others ;   and, because his triumphs here are hard earned and conscious, it is on his skill, on his rendering, that he prides himself.   The greater the painter, the less likely is he to be aware of aught else in his art than problems of rendering—but all the while he is communicating what the force of his genius makes him feel without his striving for it, almost without his being aware of it—the material and spiritual significance of forms.   However—his intimates hear from him talk of nothing but skill ;   and naturally they, and the entire public, conclude that his skill is his genius and that skill *is* art.   This, also, has at all times been the too prevalent notion of what art is, divergence of opinion existing not on the principle but on the kind of dexterity to be prized, each critic having an individual standard based always on the several peculiar problems and difficulties that interest them.   BERNARD BERENSON

(29)

It is one of the curiosities of the psychology of the artist that he is generally trying very hard to do something which has nothing to do with what he actually accomplishes ; that the fundamental quality of his work seems to come out unconsciously as a by-product of his conscious activity.   ROGER FRY

(30)

It is a fact that inductive æsthetics have not yet discovered *one single law*.

He who dispenses with doctors is prone to abandon himself to charlatans.   Thus it has befallen those who have believed in the natural laws of the beautiful.   Artists some-times adopt empirical canons, such as that of the proportions of the human body, or of the golden section, that is to say, of a line divided into two parts in such a manner that the less is to the greater as is the greater to the whole line ($bc : ab = ac : ab$).   Such canons easily become their superstitions, and they attribute to such the success of their work. Thus Michael Angelo left as a precept to his disciple Marco del Pino of Siena that " he should always make a pyramidal serpentine figure multiplied by one, two, three," a precept

---

[1] For example, compare representations of legs of standing figures in illustrations 23 and 25.

[2] " 'Form' . . . 'tactile values.'   Either refers to all the more static sources of life-enhancement, such as volume, bulk, inner substance, and texture " (p. 147, *The Northern Italian Painters of the Renaissance*, Bernard Berenson, 1907).   Modern psychology would describe the reaction to form as being more complex in character.

which did not enable Marco di Siena to emerge from that mediocrity which we can yet observe in his many works, here in Naples. Others extracted from the sayings of Michael Angelo the precept that serpentine undulating lines were the *true lines of beauty*. Whole volumes have been composed on these laws of beauty, on the golden section, and on the undulating and serpentine lines. These should, in our opinion, be looked upon as the *astrology of Æsthetic*.   CROCE

(31)

It strikes me that no good will ever come to Art, as such, from the analytic study of æsthetics—harm rather, if the abstractions could in any way be made the basis of practice. We should get stark things done on system with all the intangible personal *je ne sais quaw* left out. The difference between the first and second best things in art absolutely seems to escape definition—it is a matter of a hair, a shade, an inward quiver of some kind— yet what miles away in point of preciousness ! Absolutely the same verbal formula applies to the supreme success and to the thing that just misses it, and yet verbal formulas are all that . . . æsthetics will give.   WILLIAM JAMES

(32)

Those who have mastered the wisdom of the scientific method and are able to think scientifically experience many charming temptations. . . . Our present hot-heads want to grasp what is scientifically ungraspable ; to discover the physical laws of creative art ; to detect the general law and formula by which the artist, who feels them instinctively, creates musical compositions, pictures, novels, etc. Such formulæ probably do exist in nature. We know we can find in nature A, B, C, D, do, re, mi, fa, sol, and curves, straight lines, circles, squares, green, red, blue. We know that all this in certain combinations produces a melody, or a poem, or a picture, just as simple chemical substances in certain combinations produce a tree, a stone, or the sea. We are aware that the combination exists, but the law of the combination is hidden from us. Those who possess the scientific method feel with their souls that a musical composition and a tree have something in common, that both are created in accordance with equally regular and simple laws. Hence the question : What are these laws ? Hence the temptation to work out a physiology of creative art . . . base . . . arguments on science and the laws of nature. . . . If the critics insist upon taking their stand on scientific ground, no good will come of it ; they will waste a dozen years, write a lot of rubbish, make the question still more confusing —and get nowhere. To think scientifically is good in everything, but the trouble is that scientific speculation about creative art will sink in the end to searching for the " cells " or the " centres " which control the creative faculty. . . .

For those who are inspired by the scientific method, to whom God has granted the rare talent of thinking scientifically, there is, in my opinion, but one way out—the philosophy of creative art. It is possible to gather together all the best that has been created by artists throughout the ages, and, employing the scientific method,[1] to grasp that common element which makes them like one another and conditions their value. That common element will be the law. Works which are called immortal have a great deal in

---

[1] The method, in this instance, cannot be described as purely scientific as in the end the intuitive, rather than the reasoning faculties must be relied upon.

common ; if that common element were excluded from each of them, the work would lose its value and charm. It follows, then, that that universal element is essential, and forms the *conditio sine qua non* of every work that aspires to immortality.

TCHEKHOV

(33)

A good picture will never be produced by theories. They generally serve to disguise a poverty of means of expression. In any case they are only put together after the achievement.

RENOIR

(34)

The poetic principle, which makes the rules of poetry, is formulated and modelled after the poems are written.

BAUDELAIRE

(35)

Could a rule be given from without, poetry would cease to be poetry and sink into a mechanical art. . . . The *rules* of the imagination are themselves the very powers of growth and production. The *words* to which they are reducible present only the outlines and external appearance of the fruit.

COLERIDGE

(36)

It were as wise to cast a violet into a crucible that you might discover the formal principles of its colour and odour, as seek to transfuse from one language into another the creations of a poet.

SHELLEY

(37)

No workman whose mind I have examined is, at present, capable of design in the arts. Only of imitation, and of exquisite manual execution, such as is unsurpassable by the work of any time or country ; manual execution which, however, being wholly mechanical, is always profitless to the man himself, and profitless, ultimately, to those who possess the work.

RUSKIN

(38)

Good, or rather true, execution is that in which practice, apparently material, adds to thought, without which thought is not complete.

DELACROIX

(39)

. . . The natural impulse must arise and itself be strong enough to suggest and develop its own form. It may come to perfection only after long conscious toil and difficulty—and the sort of toil is different in the different arts. In all of them the Reason is a most active helpmate, but always the servant of the emotion. It is a mark of the consummate artist that the more he works on his production, the more he " touches it up," the more " spontaneous " it will appear. That is the object of his toil in the mastery of his material : and his conscious Reason works humbly for him in the field of æsthetics, having become, so to speak, the conscious activity of his instinct. But a lesser artist, when he seeks to better his original sketch, will ruin it by the irrelevant additions or substitutions of another mood.

ROBERT BRIDGES

(40)

But, though invention be the mother of poetry, yet the child is, like all others, born naked, and must be nourished with care, clothed with exactness and elegance, educated with industry, instructed with art, improved by application, corrected with severity, and accomplished with labour and with time, before it arrives at any great perfection or growth.

SIR WILLIAM TEMPLE

COMMENTARY

The passages quoted suggest that design results when artistic experience is symbolised, shaped, and completed through embodiment in a given medium, such as stone, pigment, wood, clay, etc. ; and that the beauty of art must be the beauty of design. The words, *a work of art*, should be taken literally. They should indicate a completed whole, built up out of different elements, and made one by the work of the art faculty.

Except in so far as an exact copy is possible, no two works of art can be alike, for no two artistic experiences can be the same, although they all share the same nature. Each is coloured by a different personality or mood ; each is expressive of a different temperament, the outcome of a given age or country, and each embodies a different reaction to a particular subject, shaped by the limitations and by the expressive powers of materials, tools, and technique. The changing aspects of life are the raw material from which the works of art are wrought. They thus portray the mind of man from age to age, his needs, his sorrow or joy, his wisdom or ignorance. In masterpieces of art precious experiences of rare minds are embodied, and through design communicated to those who can share them. In our response to works of art the greater our sensibility the more deeply aware we shall be of design and of the experience of reality which design communicates, and the more rapidly our conscious interest in other elements of the work of art will be overshadowed. The greater still contains the less, but the ultimate value of art triumphs over subordinate interests and enrichments.

To establish the unity of a work of art each element must be seen and felt in part as form (see p. 18). In a painting, for example, each head or limb, each piece of drapery, each tree, cloud, or grassy slope, must take on a certain solidity, a peculiar abstract quality, that raises it from the level of fact to a level where it exists in a new and common medium. Such elements are in this way harmonised, and are ready to be combined into a larger whole. Fig. 1[1] is an example of this power to present natural objects in terms of form. Here a baker's daughter of fourteen, a native of Cyprus, has given to her rendering of drapery, no doubt unconsciously, a plastic quality and an exquisiteness of texture only to be compared with the work of a fifteenth-century primitive. What she has drawn is far removed from the sheet which must have formed her model. We are conscious of firmness and solidity, universal qualities necessary to our being. We feel with Ruskin (see p. 4) that the least intrusion of an exact rendering of the object drawn would spoil our pleasure. The contrasts shown in Figs. 2–4 should make this matter still clearer. A child's beauty is felt equally in both Figs. 3 and 4, but in the work of art all the softness, roundness, and delicate curves of the shapes of nature have taken on this plastic and semi-abstract character, and by these means a sense of heightened reality is communicated. In Fig. 2 we fail to find either the impersonal reflection of natural beauty, or the enduring beauty and vitality of art. We have instead a somewhat sentimental illustration.

The artist is necessarily excited and inspired by his subject-matter. Without the stimulus and variety offered by contact with nature and with the world about him, his work would tend to become monotonous and devitalised, and would grow too subjective in character. But it is imperative that he should conceive his subject in terms of design. In this way, the permanent element of art will ultimately prevail, and the subject-matter, which at first may so deeply interest both artist and

[1] See Frontispiece.

spectator, will cease to be the true subject-matter of the work of art because it will give place to a sense of something universal, although the work will always retain its individual character.

In each work, the conception of the elements and the arrangement of the whole are carried on together. In Fig. 38 we find a definite formal arrangement, and the sincerity which must form the basis of all art, but when we compare this picture with Fig. 39 we realise that the subject-matter has not been completely transmuted into form. In Fig. 39, both the appearance of the figures and the pathos of the scene have been completely absorbed into design. Emotional intensity is expressed in both pictures, but in Fig. 38 the emotion is limited to the occasion described, while in Fig. 39 it takes on a universal character. Grief and pain are lost in an underlying and transfiguring harmony, order, and significance.[1]

Composition that is design, and composition that is not design, are clearly shown in Figs. 35 and 36. In the decoration of both bowls we are conscious of order and purpose and the desire to create formal significance, but whereas in the first we have a beautiful example of the sensitiveness and rhythmic vitality of art, in the second we are only too painfully aware of the absence of these qualities, and of a mechanical labouring after design. In the first bowl we can almost see the pattern move as it makes its delicate adjustments to the undulation of the vessel, but in the second the lifeless patterns are plastered on the surface without any response to the suggestions of its curves. There is no design because there has not been the experience that is the mother of design.

As a contrast to these two bowls, Fig. 37 can be studied. Here we have a vessel cut from an agate. The veinings in the stone have no purpose in their disposition, and, though decorative in their effect, they appeal to our senses only as do the stripes on a zebra or the markings on a butterfly's wing. The forms of nature can never convey to us that sense of individual mind and purpose peculiar to the ordered forms of art. A full appreciation of the differences between these three bowls will lay a firm foundation for an understanding of art as a whole.[2]

Let no one carry away the idea that in design we always find an obviously geometric balance round a central point. Design of this nature is common, but there is a subtler type which may embody a mathematical relationship, though it might be difficult or impossible to prove it. This type of design will be discussed later. As examples of it, Figs. 48 and 83 may be mentioned. The cohesion and equilibrium of the parts must be *felt* by the whole being.

In illustration of the passage from Delacroix's Journal, quoted on p. 16, Figs. 40–43 may be studied. Here we can see examples of the relation between a great painter's sketch and his finished picture as inspired by the sketch. Fig. 40 is one of three studies made by Claude for the picture illustrated in Fig. 41.

[1] Compare the well-known words of Aristotle : " Poetry is something more philosophic and of graver import than history, since its statements are of the nature rather of universals, whereas those of history are singulars." Also the following passage by Schopenhauer : " Music . . . never expresses the phenomenon, but only the inner nature. . . . It does not therefore express this or that particular and definite joy, this or that sorrow, or pain, or horror, or delight, or merriment, or peace of mind ; but joy, sorrow, pain, horror, delight, merriment, peace of mind *themselves*, to a certain extent in the abstract, their abstract nature, without accessories and therefore without their motives. Yet we completely understand them in this quintessence.

[2] Many examples of painting, sculpture, and other forms of art have been made with definite reference to their place in larger schemes of design. When such a unit has been removed from its surroundings, it may lose something of the significance it gained by its incorporation, or by the effect produced upon it by its original lighting. It may also be out of harmony with its new environment. Nevertheless it must be judged on the artistic qualities it possesses in itself, apart from any enhancement due to connection with, or subordination to, a larger whole. The artistic value of the examples of architecture given is to be judged without reference to climate and civic and rural background. We do not wish to deprecate the great importance of larger harmonies, but we are anxious to dispel the illusion, so frequently met, that a unit that lacks design can acquire design by some felicitous insertion in a larger whole. A bad frieze or picture in a museum was always a bad frieze or picture, no matter from what building it came. Allowance must of course be made at times for distortions and exaggerations deliberately introduced by the artist to counteract effects arising from the special position his work was to occupy. A statue originally designed to be seen from below may exemplify this, or a painting taken from a ceiling.

CHAPTER III

ANALYSIS OF DESIGN (a)

*A*RGUMENT.—*The artist is conscious of the fundamental forms which underlie the appearances of objects. In his art he suggests these forms, and gives to his work a certain abstract quality which exists in, and through, the inherent interest of the subject-matter (other than form and arrangements of form) of the work of art. These fundamental forms are not in themselves works of art, but are an important part of the raw material out of which a work of art is made.*

(41)

The genuinely healthy child will be always active, he will employ himself. Why? He wishes to make something so that his inward desire may also appear externally. He wishes that what is hidden within him, and lives in him, may also outwardly exist. . . .

But now what is the further cause of all activity in the child? It is just life, as life is the first cause of all existence in God. Therefore the child invests with life whatever he sees—that is, he not only anticipates, feels, and experiences life in all, but he even attributes conscious life, will-power—conscious, self-determining will-power—to all. . . .

. . . Let us now observe and question the child himself, and see what he chooses in his earliest period of development for a counterpart of himself and of his efforts. It is the simplest inanimate object but also (a highly remarkable fact) the heaviest. He prefers wood and stones. . . .

. . . Weight attraction is the first expression of the power, as it were, the life in Nature which expresses itself in its higher degree as the attraction of the senses; and in its purer development, as a spiritual attraction, as love. . . .

. . . For his freest development he likes best the ball. Just the ball is demonstratively the middle point and point of union, I may say the representation of all for which the child strives as a counterpart for his self-development and cultivation. It shows completeness in itself, and is yet the general representative of all things—of rest and movement, of totality and unity, of that which is all-sided and that which has but one surface. It unites in itself the visible and the invisible (its middle and axis, etc.). By the ball, the child can now accomplish and represent unnumbered things which exist within him as desire, idea, and thought. And, with the ball, the child can imitate innumerable things which he sees around him. . . .

What is now to be the indispensably necessary advance to the next plaything? . . . On account of the plurality of its properties the cube, in companion with the simple round sphere, shows and gives a plurality of use and a multiplicity of the most different appearances—as the sphere shows an all-sidedness of movement. Thus the always stable cube, with its straight surfaces, represents itself to the child as the opposite of the round, easily movable sphere, but yet similar to it. . . .

By its form it leads *firstly* to the perception of the solid form, and to the knowledge of its boundaries, of the sides, the edges, and the corners (surfaces, lines, points), and of their different relations to one another in form, position, and size. . . .

Form, size, and number are important to the comprehension of the figure and to the perception of its interior, and are therefore important to life. . . . With the human being as a child, everything begins in, and with, the comprehension of what is perceived by the senses. . . . The cube serves as an introduction into life and to the objects of life by the different ways of perceiving and looking at it, which proceed from the child's fancy ; for example, as a square stone, a bale of goods, as a chopping block, as a tree tub in a greenhouse, etc. . . .

The child likes best that plaything, whatever its outward appearance may be, by which and with which he can form and accomplish the most—that is, can call forth in himself the greater number of and most satisfying conceptions, imaginations, and fancies, as vividly as if he saw them actually in himself, and outside of himself, even in the most imperfect outlines and representations. . . .

The law of connections is the most important law of the universe, of humanity, and of life in general. . . . The sphere and the cube are pure opposites. They stand to each other in the relation of unity and plurality, but especially of movement and rest, of round and straight. The law of connection demands for these two opposite yet like bodies and objects of play a connecting one, which is the cylinder. It combines unity complete in itself in the round surface, and plurality in the two straight ones . . . the cylinder combines plane and round. . . . Consider how the country children play with the cylindrical or round pieces of wood. . . .

By means of this manifestation of form and movements these solids, and the play with them, give many opportunities for the observation and consideration of form, size, and number (particularly in a somewhat advanced stage of childhood), and in many ways introduce the child into the phenomena of Nature and life around him. . . .

The connection of the spherical and the rectangular has for the child the expression of the human. . . . If a man comprehends fundamentally and in all its relations, for example, the ball, the sphere, and the cube (which are indeed only one in three), as representative of the normal and fundamental perception of all that occupies space, and of what is given and demanded thereby, he will thus become capable of recognising, observing, and handling easily also all other things, even that which stands alone, yet is the same in all its bearings and relations, for he learns to see the manifold in the single plurality in unity, and *vice versa* . . . and should find this out in his life. . . .

FROEBEL

(42)

Who first called his attention to the pyramid, cube, etc., I do not know. He may have seen an account of them, by chance, in a book. But the fact remains that at this early time his fancy, like that of the old Greek geometers, was arrested by these types of complete symmetry : and his imagination so thoroughly mastered them that he proceeded to make them with his own hand. That he himself attached more importance to this moment than the letter indicates is proved by the care with which he has preserved these perishable things, so that they (or those which replaced them in 1848) are still in existence after thirty-seven years.

CAMPBELL *and* GARNETT (*on James Clerk Maxwell, aged 13*)

(43)

There is a certain pattern of charm and beauty which consists in a certain relation between our nature . . . and the thing which pleases us. Everything formed on this pattern pleases us, whether it be a house, song, discourse, poetry, prose, woman, birds, rivers, trees, rooms, dress, etc. Anything not according to this pattern displeases those who have good taste. . . . There is a perfect relation between a song and a house which are made on a good pattern, because they are like this good pattern, though each after its kind.

PASCAL

(44)

Vitruvius, the ancient architect, whom the Romans employed upon great buildings, says that whosoever desires to build should study the perfection of the human figure, for in it are discovered the most secret mysteries of proportion. So, before I say anything about architecture, I will state how a well-formed man should be made, and then about a woman, a child, and a horse. . . .

ALBRECHT DÜRER

(45)

Geometric figures are naturally more beautiful than other irregular ; in this all consent as to a law of Nature. Of geometrical Figures the square and the circle are most beautiful. . . .

There are only two beautiful Positions of straight Lines, perpendicular and horizontal ; this is from Nature and consequently Necessity, no other than upright being firm.

SIR CHRISTOPHER WREN

(46)

One thing I have come to realise is that geometry is at the bottom of sentiment, or rather that each expression of a sentiment is made by a movement which geometry governs. Geometry, indeed, is everywhere present in nature. Why, then, should it not be so in the raising of an arm or another instinctive movement of a limb ? A woman combing her hair goes through a series of rhythmic movements which constitute a beautiful harmony—a grace of the highest order. The entire rhythm of the body is governed by law. The body cannot uncentre itself. It remains in union with all that composes it, and acts in conjunction with its environment.

Nature is the supreme architect. Everything is built in the finest equilibrium, and everything too is enclosed in a triangle, or a cube, or some modification of them.

RODIN

(47)

All sensuous magnitudes are either in space (extended magnitudes) or in time (numeral magnitudes). . . . Heights appear altogether more sublime than equally great lengths, the reason of which lies partly in the fact that dynamical sublimity is associated with the aspect of the first. A simple length, however immeasurable it may be, has nothing fearful in itself, but a height certainly has, since we might be precipitated from it. For the same reason depth is still more sublime than height, since the idea of the fearful is closely united with it.   SCHILLER

(48)

Imitation—it enters the very fastnesses of Character ; and we—our souls—ourselves —are for ever imitating what we see and hear, the forms, the sounds, which haunt our memories, our imagination. We imitate not only if we play a part on the stage, but when we sit as spectators, while our thoughts follow the acting of another ; while we read Homer, and put ourselves lightly, fluently, into the place of those he describes ; we imitate unconsciously the line and colour of the walls around us, the trees of the wayside, the animals we pet or make use of, the very dress we wear.   PATER

(49)

Æsthetic beauty in a building is essentially the same as that of sculpture, and results from the expression of a plastic idea. This expression of a plastic idea is very rare in our architecture, and almost unknown in our sculpture.

I come to much the most difficult part of my task here—how to explain what I understand by a plastic idea. I mean something like this, for in attempting so difficult a task I shall very likely fail to give any precise verbal definition. I shall certainly be ready to accept any suggested improvements which will make the sense more clear. I mean, then, such a construction of three-dimensional shapes as satisfies the contemplation of their relations to one another and to the whole combination. Let me suppose I take a number of half-spheres of different sizes and put them in turn on the top of a cube. Let us suppose both an artist and a mathematician to be assisting at this experiment. We may suppose, for the sake of argument, that our mathematician or logical contemplator finds that one particular-sized hemisphere gives rise, in relation to the cube, to peculiar and interesting mathematical properties. Our artist or sensual contemplator might also find that a certain size of hemisphere gave, in relation to the cube, a satisfaction quite different from that which could be got from the other combinations. It might even be that he and the mathematician would find that it was the same particular hemisphere which satisfied each of them. But this would be merely an interesting fact for a psychologist, it would not affect in any way the nature of the artist's satisfaction, which is immediate and direct, and of a totally different kind from the mathematician's interest. What we have, then, to recognise is that certain relations of solid shapes to each other do set up in the mind which contemplates them a peculiar condition of tension and equilibrium, which is the essence of the æsthetic emotion. And an object which has these relations that are satisfactory to æsthetic contemplation may be said to have plastic form.

Now it is evident that an object may be in three dimensions without having in this sense three-dimensional or plastic form. In fact, all buildings, as all sculpture, is three-dimensional, has mass and volume, but it may not have what I call three-dimensional form. That is to say, the relations of its parts together may be merely casual, the result of accident or outward necessity, and not self-explanatory, and apparently necessitated to the imagination.

It is clear that an architect's choice of plastic forms is not free. It is limited sharply by practical conditions. But he has generally at his disposal the rectangular block (I believe this is more properly called a rectangular parallelopiped), of which the cube is one variety, the cylinder, the hemisphere, the pyramid, and the prism, or sections of these forms. Now the perfectly lucid expression of most of these forms on a considerable scale has already a certain effect on the imagination. The Pyramids are a good example. I have never seen them, but I can quite believe they possess a crude impressiveness. Ruskin somewhere describes approaching a town at dusk and being thrilled by the vision of what looked like a vast Temple of Vesta until, on nearer approach, he saw a gasometer, whereupon he delivers a tirade against modern iniquity. He was really impressed by a bare cylinder on a large scale, but his morbid historico-social over-sensitiveness prevented him from recognising that what had impressed his imagination through his senses was so far as it went beautiful, and that its beauty ought not really to be spoilt by the unpleasant overtones of association. Or, again, the sheer undisturbed rectangular mass of a factory may, if its relation to the earth surface is fortunate, give one a sensation of the kind I mean.

But so far we are dealing only with the raw material out of which the language of plastic design in architecture can be made. It is when such forms are combined, when the superposition or interpenetration of two or more rectangular blocks, or of blocks with sections of cylinders, and so forth, is devised in relation to the earth surface and its possible plastic arrangement, that we begin to get the essentially æsthetic quality of architecture. Or, rather, when such interplay of these elemental forms is perfectly adjusted to the expression of an idea. How rare or how common this is will, I suppose, be a matter for infinite discussion. In such a matter it would be ridiculous to suppose one could prove anything. One can only keep one's sensitiveness alert and one's mind free from prejudice and record one's impressions as honestly as possible. Clearly the sensibility to such plastic form varies immensely with individuals (at least as much as their ears for musical relations), and still more, perhaps, the assiduity and persistence of their contemplation of such plastic ideas.

ROGER FRY

(50)

Æsthetic satisfaction . . . always depends upon the apprehension of a (Platonic) Idea. For architecture, considered merely as a fine art, the Ideas of the lowest grades of nature, such as gravity, rigidity, and cohesion, are the peculiar theme ; but not, as has hitherto been assumed, merely regular form, proportion, and symmetry, which, as something purely geometrical, properties of space, are not Ideas, and therefore cannot be the theme of a fine art. Thus in architecture also, they are of secondary origin, and have a subordinate significance, which I shall bring out immediately. . . . Works of architecture, in order to act æsthetically, absolutely must have a considerable size . . . because only great masses make the action of gravitation apparent and impressive in a high degree. . . . The tendency and antagonism of those fundamental forces of nature constitute the special æsthetical material of architecture, which, according to its nature, requires large masses in order to become visible, and indeed capable of being felt. . . . Architecture acts primarily in our spatial perception and accordingly appeals to our *a priori* faculty for this. But these qualities only result from the greatest regularity of the forms and rationality of their relations. Therefore beautiful architecture selects only regular figures composed of straight lines, or regular curves, and also the bodies which result from these, such as cubes, parallelopipeda, cylinders, spheres, pyramids, and cones, but as openings sometimes circles or ellipses, yet as a rule quadrates, and still oftener rectangles. . . . Only by means of symmetry does a work of architecture announce itself as an individual unity, and as the development of a central thought.

. . . The conflict between gravity and rigidity is the whole æsthetic material of architecture. . . . The whole mass of the building, if left to its original tendency, would exhibit a mere heap or clump, bound as closely as possible to the earth. . . . The beauty, at any rate of a building, lies in the obvious adaptation of every part, not to the outward arbitrary end of man (so far the work belongs to practical architecture), but directly to the stability of the whole, to which the position, dimensions, and form of every part must have so necessary a relation that were it possible, if one part were taken away, the whole would fall to pieces. . . .

Architecture . . . affects us dynamically, and what speaks to us through it is not mere form and symmetry, but rather those fundamental forces of nature. . . .

SCHOPENHAUER

(51)

Psychology has ascertained that sight alone gives no accurate sense of the third dimension. In our infancy, long before we are conscious of the process, the sense of touch, helped by muscular sensations of movement, teaches us to appreciate depth, the third dimension, both in objects and in space.

In the same unconscious years we learn to make of touch, of the third dimension, the test of reality. The child is still dimly aware of the intimate connection between touch and the third dimension. He cannot persuade himself of the unreality of Looking-Glass Land until he has touched the back of the mirror. Later, we entirely forget the connection, although it remains true, that every time our eyes recognise reality we are, as a matter of fact, giving tactile values to retinal impressions.[1]

Now painting is an art which aims at giving an abiding impression of artistic reality with only two dimensions. The painter must, therefore, do consciously what we all do unconsciously—construct his third dimension, and he can accomplish his task only as we accomplish ours, by giving tactile values to retinal impressions.

. . . *Unless* it satisfies our tactile imagination, a picture will not exert the fascination of an ever-heightened reality ; first we shall exhaust its ideas, and then its power of

[1] See footnote 2, p. 19.

appealing to our emotions, and its "beauty" will not seem more significant at the thousandth look than at the first.

BERNARD BERENSON

(52)

Even at Mass the painter did not cease to dream of his painting. A young artist had made the journey to Aix in the hope of seeing him. It was Sunday. As the weather was bad, a friend, who was directing him, naturally took him to Saint-Sauveur, at the moment when every one was streaming out after Mass. When he pointed out Cézanne, the young artist made straight for him. Finding no way of escape Cézanne appeared as startled as a sleeper suddenly awakened ; and in nervousness, let his prayer book fall. But when the other told him that he was a painter : " Ah, you are one of us ? " cried Cézanne, becoming at once very affable, and seizing him brusquely by the button of his jacket : " Listen an instant : everything in nature is spherical or cylindrical."

VOLLARD on CÉZANNE

(53)

Treat nature in terms of the cylinder, the sphere, and the cone, and put them all into perspective so that every side of an object or plane is oriented towards a central point. The lines parallel to the horizon give breadth. . . . Lines perpendicular to this horizon give depth ; and nature, for us men, is felt in depth rather than as a surface. . . . I was an impressionist . . . but I wanted to make out of impressionism something solid and enduring, like the art of the museums.

CÉZANNE

(54)

The question of the *beauty of geometrical figures* is connected with æsthetic Physic. But if by geometrical figures be understood the concepts of geometry, the concept of the triangle, the square, the cone, these are neither beautiful nor ugly : they are concepts. If, on the other hand, by such figures we understood bodies which possess definite geometrical forms, these will be ugly or beautiful, like every natural fact, according to the ideal connexions in which they are placed.

CROCE

COMMENTARY

The meaning of these quotations dealing with fundamental geometric forms is so clear that the illustrations need little commentary. In Fig. 44 is a building that has much of the impressiveness of a great temple, yet it was probably erected without conscious artistic aim, for it is an American grain elevator. It owes its impressiveness to the bold use of cube and cylinder, and to the happy adjustment of their proportions, whether intended or not. Each must judge for himself if it gives him the experience of art. Probably most people will feel in it a certain lack of refinement.

But when we turn to Fig. 45 there can be no doubt that the building shown is a work of art. The significance of the elemental forms has not been lost in an overgrowth of detail, and the purpose of the artist is communicated through balance of volume and beauty of line. In Fig. 46 we see the crude impressiveness of the pyramid and the cylinder. Here, again, these forms are not found in the ideal connections of art to which Croce referred, though the crenelations of the gateway have probably artistic as well as military purpose. In Fig. 47 we feel the pyramid and its sections underlying the form of a mediæval barn, and our pleasure in the building is probably due to a conscious or unconscious recognition of its fundamental character. But as in the case of the grain elevator, each must decide for himself, if the barn can be described as a work of art. In Figs. 48–50 we enjoy the cube, the cylinder, the pyramid, and the sphere or their sections, held in equilibrium and charged with the creative purpose of the architect.

Figs. 51 and 53 present a bowl and a vase, but beneath the shapes that meet the eye, and our consciousness of their power to be filled and to contain, we feel the simple yet exquisitely sensitive rendering of sphere or cylinder or their sections. Fig. 52 displays the savage's sense of these forms as the basis of the human body. The heads of the absorbed debaters are represented by simple hemi-spheres : the bodies and limbs by cylinders. Figs. 54 and 55 show two figures each obviously composed in three dimensions. Yet when we contrast these pieces of sculpture, we see how all sense of the solidity of the underlying geometric forms has been lost in the modern statue. The power to suggest these forms is deplorably lacking in the work of almost all modern sculptors.

CHAPTER IV

ANALYSIS OF DESIGN (*b*)

ARGUMENT.—There are elements in design which affect us emotionally.

(55)

Let us now see how the artist passes from the stage of merely gratifying our demand for sensuous order and variety to that where he arouses our emotions. I will call the various methods by which this is effected the emotional elements of design.

The first element is that of the rhythm of the line with which the forms are delineated.

The drawn line is the record of a gesture, and that gesture is modified by the artist's feeling, which is thus communicated to us directly.[1]

The second element is mass. When an object is so represented that we recognise it as having inertia we feel its power of resisting movement, or communicating its own movement to other bodies, and our imaginative reaction to such an image is governed by our experience of mass in actual life.

The third element is space. The same sized square on two pieces of paper can be made by very simple means to appear to represent either a cube two or three inches high, or a cube of hundreds of feet, and our reaction to it is proportionately changed.

The fourth element is that of light and shade. Our feelings towards the same object become totally different according as we see it strongly illuminated against a black background or dark against light.

The fifth element is that of colour. That this has a direct emotional effect is evident from such words as "gay," "dull," "melancholy" in relation to colour.

I would suggest the possibility of another element, though perhaps it is only a compound of mass and space : it is that of the inclination to the eye of a plane, whether it is impending over or leaning away from us.

Now it will be noticed that nearly all these emotional elements of design are connected with essential conditions of our physical existence : rhythm appeals to all the sensations which accompany muscular activity ; mass to all the infinite adaptations to the force of gravity which we are forced to make ; the spatial judgment is equally profound and universal in its application to life ; our feeling about inclined planes is connected with our necessary judgments about the conformation of the earth itself ; light, again, is so necessary a condition of our existence that we become intensely sensitive

---

[1] For further analysis of line, see *Vision and Design*, by Roger Fry, p. 160.

to changes in its intensity. Colour is the only one of our elements which is not of critical or universal importance to life, and its emotional effect is neither so deep nor so clearly determined as the others. It will be seen, then, that the graphic arts arouse emotions in us by playing upon what one may call the overtones of some of our primary physical needs. They have, indeed, this great advantage over poetry, that they can appeal more directly and immediately to the emotional accompaniment of our bare physical existence.

I have admitted that there is beauty in Nature, that is to say, that certain objects constantly do, and perhaps any object may, compel us to regard it with that intense disinterested contemplation that belongs to the imaginative life, and which is impossible to the actual life of necessity and action ; but that in objects created to arouse the æsthetic feeling we have an added consciousness of purpose on the part of the creator, that he made it on purpose not to be used but to be regarded and enjoyed ; and that this feeling is characteristic of the æsthetic judgment proper.

When the artist passes from pure sensations to emotions aroused by means of sensations, he uses natural forms which, in themselves, are calculated to move our emotions, and he presents these in such a manner that the forms themselves generate in us emotional states, based upon the fundamental necessities of our physical and physiological nature. The artist's attitude to natural form is, therefore, infinitely various according to the emotions he wishes to arouse. He may require for his purpose the most complete representation of a figure, he may be intensely realistic, provided that his presentment, in spite of its closeness to natural appearance, disengages clearly for us the appropriate emotional elements. Or he may give us the merest suggestion of natural forms, and rely almost entirely upon the force and intensity of the emotional elements involved in his presentment.

We may, then, dispense once for all with the idea of likeness to Nature, of correctness or incorrectness as a test, and consider only whether the emotional elements inherent in natural form are adequately discovered, unless, indeed, the emotional idea depends at any point upon likeness, or completeness, or representation. ROGER FRY

(56)

What kind of intellect must he have who sees only the colours of things and not the forms of things ? WILLIAM BLAKE

(57)

All men, completely organised and justly tempered, enjoy colour ; it is meant for the perpetual comfort and delight of the human heart : it is richly bestowed on the highest works of creation and is the eminent sign and seal of perfection in them ; being associated with *life* in the human body, with *light* in the sky, with *purity* and hardness in the earth —death, night, and pollution of all kinds being colourless. And although if form and colour be brought into complete opposition, so that it should be put to us as a matter of stern choice whether we should have a work of art all of form, without colour (as an Albert Dürer engraving), or all of colour, without form (as an imitation of mother-of-

3

pearl), form is beyond all comparison the more precious of the two ; and in explaining the essence of objects, form is essential, and colour more or less accidental.

RUSKIN

(58)

Colourists design as nature designs : their forms find their natural limits in the harmonious strife of coloured masses.

As a dream exists in an atmosphere which forms a part of it, so, in the same way, a conception that has become a composition must move in coloured surroundings which are peculiar to it. The art of the colourist is allied, in certain of its aspects, to mathematics and to music.

BAUDELAIRE

(59)

Colour enhances painting ; but she is only a lady-in-waiting, because all she does is to make still more attractive the true perfections of art.

INGRES

COMMENTARY

The sensitive and expressive qualities of line can be observed in Figs. 56 and 57. We need not be told that the first script is the outcome of a primitive mind, and the second of a mind that is the product of many more centuries of civilisation. Figs. 59 and 60 show the sensitive employment of line in objects of use, the simple expressions of equally simple experiences, while in Fig. 58 we find line that is tending to become shape, while still retaining its linear character. Figs. 61 and 62 show subtler communications of more complex experiences. The line in the sketch of the bodies seems to run from the pen of its author as liquid energy. In Fig. 61 we have line that is expressive of the limitations of mass rather than line expressive in itself, although it has an exquisite sensitiveness of its own. Fig. 63 represents the forcible and vital line of an early Chinese draughtsman ; Fig. 64 the rhythmic beauty of linear form in a completed picture. Every part conveys movement suspended for ever by the magic of art. Figs. 65 and 66 are examples of the employment of line in the structure of a Baroque façade and in architectural ornament. Lastly, in contrast with all these examples of rhythmic and vital line, reference should be made to Fig. C, Plate LI. The line in this drawing is utterly mechanical and inexpressive. Many of its curves might have been produced by compasses.

The power to suggest mass, and the lack of that power, are evident in Figs. 69 and 70, which reproduce two houses facing each other across a street. Both houses are, of course, built of solid units, yet nearly all sense of solidity has been lost in Fig. 70. The case is parallel to that of the two pieces of sculpture in Figs. 54 and 55. Fig. 68 shows us the quality of mass in ornament. In Fig. 67 we find the same emphasis in sculpture. The toad has the bulk and impressiveness of a mountain. The paintings of Giotto (see Fig. 71) have been analysed so often that they need not be discussed here. Mr. Berenson has described the hieratic dignity and gravity that invest the figures of the master through the suggested weight and density of their formal presentation, and the emphasised recession of their planes. So solid are the forms they might be sculptured stone. It is comforting to find that the work of a living painter (Fig. 72) can exist in company with the work of so great a master without annihilation. Fig. 73 shows a plastic and monumental treatment of a bunch of flowers by the man who styled himself the first primitive of the new movement in art. The interest of each flower is in every instance subordinated to the interests of the mass, and the mass is given a density which few flower painters have achieved. The modern flower painter cannot study this picture too closely.

The suggestion of space (or the lack of it) in painting can be studied in Figs. 74 and 75. Here we can see that this sense does not necessarily result from correct perspective. In Fig. 75, owing to the subtle relationship set up between the planes, space takes on the solidity of a cube. In Fig. 74, however, although the perspective is correct, there is little sense of depth.[1] Space wisely handled in architecture is illustrated in Fig. 76. As an example of the different effects produced upon us by the varying aspects of the same subject-matter, according to its presentation in light or shade, Figs. 77 and 78 may be compared.

The fifth element of colour cannot, unfortunately, be studied in this book, except in so far as black and white are colours. But the fact that we can get a very fair idea of the value of a work of art from a photograph or from a half-tone reproduction should be considered in this connection. Certain colours, when related, may harmonise or clash, but in art, as the passages quoted point out, colour can only become significant in relation to form. The great colourist will conceive his design as a relationship of coloured planes. A lack of colour harmony will spoil the unity of a design. But colours, in themselves, have a strong effect upon the senses and are one of the most important raw materials that the artist can command.

As regards the possible sixth emotional element in design, each can study the illustrations for himself and take his own decision.

[1] See p. 41 for discussion of space-composition.

CHAPTER V

ANALYSIS OF DESIGN (c)

ARGUMENT.—*Line, mass, space, light and shade, and colour, are united in the rhythmic order of design. Inherent in these forms, influencing them, and influenced by them, may be subject-matter other than design. But eluding all analysis the informing spirit of art escapes us and remains indefinable.*

(60)

The arrangement of colours and lines is an art analogous to the composition of music, and entirely independent of the representation of facts. Good colouring does not necessarily convey the image of anything but itself. It consists in certain proportions and arrangements of rays of light, but not in likeness to anything. A few touches of certain greys and purples laid by a master's hand on white paper will be good colouring; as more touches are added beside them we may find out that they were intended to represent a dove's neck, and we may praise, as the drawing advances, the perfect imitation of the dove's neck. But the good colouring does not consist in that imitation but in the abstract qualities and relations of the grey and purple.

In like manner, as soon as a great sculptor begins to shape his work out of the block, we shall see that its lines are nobly arranged and of noble character. We may not have the slightest idea for what the forms are intended, whether they are of man or beast, of vegetation or drapery. Their likeness to anything does not affect their nobleness. They are magnificent forms, and that is all that we need care to know about them, in order to say whether the workman is a good or bad sculptor.

Now the noblest art is an exact unison of the abstract value, with the imitative power, of forms and colours. It is the noblest composition, used to express the noblest facts. But the human mind cannot in general unite the two perfections; it either pursues the fact to the neglect of the composition, or pursues the composition to the neglect of the fact.

And it is intended by the Deity that it *should* do this: the best art is not always wanted. Facts are often wanted, without art, as in a geological diagram; and art often without facts, as in a Turkey carpet. And most men have been made capable of giving either one or the other, but not both; only one or two, the very highest, can give both.

Observe them. Men are universally divided, as respects their artistic qualifications, into three great classes: a right, a left, and a centre. On the right side are the men of facts, on the left the men of design, in the centre the men of both.

36

The three classes, of course, pass into each other by imperceptible graduations. The men of facts are hardly ever without powers of design ; the men of design are always in some measure cognizant of facts ; and as each class possesses more or less of the powers of the opposite one, it approaches to the character of the central class. Few men, even in that central rank, are so exactly throned on the summit of the crest that they cannot be perceived to incline in the least one way or another, embracing both horizons with their glance. Now each of these classes has, as I have said, a healthy function in the world, and correlative diseases, or unhealthy functions ; and, when the work of either of them is seen in its morbid condition, we are apt to find fault with the class of workman, instead of finding fault only with the particular abuse which has permeated their action. . . .

What, then, are the diseased operations to which the three classes of workman are liable ?

Primarily two : affecting the two inferior classes :

> First. When either of these two classes Despises the other.
> Second. When either of these two classes Envies the other ; producing therefore four forms of dangerous error.

First, when the men of facts despise design. This is the error of common Dutch painters, of merely imitative painters of still life, flowers, etc., and other men who, having either the gift of accurate imitation or strong sympathies with nature, suppose all is done when the imitation is perfected, or sympathy expressed. A large body of English landscapists come into this class, including most clever sketchers from nature, who fancy that to get a sky of true tone, and a gleam of sunshine or sweep of clouds faithfully expressed, is all that can be required of art. These men are generally themselves answerable for much of their deadness of feeling to the higher qualities of composition. They probably have not originally the high gifts of design, but they lose such powers as they originally possessed by the despising, and refusing to study, the results of great power of design in others. Their knowledge, so far as it goes, being accurate, they are usually presumptuous and self-conceited, and gradually become incapable of admiring anything but what is like their own work. . . .

The second form of error is when men of design despise facts. All noble design must deal with facts to a certain extent, for there is no food for it but in nature . . . and if in the delight of inventing fantastic colour and form, the truths of nature are wilfully neglected, the intellect becomes comparatively decrepit. . . .

The third form of error is when the men of facts envy design ; that is to say, when having only imitative powers, they refuse to employ those powers upon the visible world around them ; but, having been taught that composition is the end of art, strive to obtain the inventive powers which nature has denied them, study nothing but the works of reputed designers, and perish in a fungus growth of plagiarism and laws of art. . . .

The fourth form of error is when the men of design envy facts ; that is to say, when the temptation of closely imitating nature leads them to forget their own proper ornamental function, and when they lose the power of the composition for the sake of graphic truth. . . .

The morbid state of the men of design injures themselves only ; . . . but the modern

English fact-hunter, despising design, wants to destroy everything, and becomes the most dangerous and despicable of iconoclasts, excited by egotism, instead of religion. . . .

. . . It is evident that the men of the central class cannot be liable to any morbid operation of this kind, they possessing the powers of both.   RUSKIN

(61)

By decoration I mean all those elements in a work of art which appeal directly to the senses, such as Colour and Tone, or directly stimulate ideated sensations, such as Form and Movement. . . .

Illustration . . . is all that which, in a work of art, is not Decorative.

Illustration is everything which in a work of art appeals to us, not for any intrinsic quality, as for colour or form or composition, contained in the work of art itself, but for the value the thing represented has elsewhere, whether in the world outside or in the mind within. If a work of art have no intrinsic value whatever, or if we fail to perceive it, for us it is nothing but an illustration, and it does not matter whether it be drawn, engraved or coloured on sheets of paper, or painted on a panel or wall. Raphael and Michael Angelo, Leonardo and Giorgione, if we perceive in them no qualities except such as, in the realm of actual or ideal things, belong to the images set down in their paintings, are as much mere Illustrators as the hacks who furnish designs for the popular press. In the domain of illustrations there are, it is true, whole universes of difference between the illustrations of the great men just named and the illustrations of the nameless folk of to-day, but from this point of view they are all illustrators. . . .

It is no academic reason which has led me at the opening of a small book . . . to distinguish clearly in a work of art between Decoration and Illustration. It is a steep short cut—would we had had the leisure to build a broad, gently climbing highway !— which, once bravely over, places us where we shall understand a great deal that otherwise would have for ever puzzled and perplexed us.

What is more perplexing, for example, than the veerings of fashion, or even of taste ? It makes scornful sceptics of most, and forces upon the few who still believe the alternative of silence or paradox. . . . One thing at least must be made clear at once. It is this. The question of preference in art is not at all the same that it is in life. Life makes different demands from generation to generation, from decade to decade, from year to year, nay, from day to day, from hour to hour. Our attention is stretched with the utmost interest toward those things that will help us to satisfy these demands, and with admiration toward those of our fellows who, without crowding or hindering us, have perfectly satisfied them. As the demands, so the objects of our desires and our admiration vary. And as the objects of our desire and admiration are altered, so will the subject-matter of the arts change. It cannot be otherwise. But depth of conception and attractiveness of ideal are, as we have seen, all that the greater number of even cultivated people care for in the arts ; and this being so, art must either present the current conceptions and ideal, or fail of a result in which even a restricted public will take an interest. Now the fluctuation of the ideal can affect those elements only in the work of art in which the ideal can be obviously manifest—in the Illustrative part. But this, we have agreed, is far from being the whole or even the most essential factor in art. There remain all the Decorative elements which mere change in ideal cannot touch, for the good reason that the ideal can be adequately presented without them. All therefore in the work of art which distinguishes it from the mere mental image, all the Decorative elements, the more essential elements, as I believe, are above the revolutions of fashion and taste. Ages may arise which lack even the few who in better periods have a feeling for art, as distinct from Illustration or dexterity, and they are the ages of bad taste—not of different taste. . . . The truth is that the elements essential to a painting as a work of art are beyond their perception, and that they look in a picture for nothing but a representation of something that would please them in actual life, or perhaps for the exhibition of a kind of skill that they happen to appreciate. (There are a thousand standards whereby one's tastes in matters of actual life may be judged, but as none of them are purely artistic, they are not my concern just here.)

Thus our rough division of the elements that constitute the work of art and divide it into two classes, the one Illustrative and the other Decorative, has already been of service. It has enabled us to distinguish what is subject to change and fashion from what is permanent in the work of art. The Decorative elements, the intrinsic values, are as perdurable as the psychic processes themselves, which, as we have reason to believe, vary only in degree from age to age, but in kind remain the same through all times. But illustration changes from epoch to epoch with the contents of the mind, the visual part of which it reproduces, and it is as varied as are races and individuals.

It follows then that an age of art which contains few if any except illustrative elements will tend to pass away with the ideals it reproduces ; also that if we do not perceive the Decorative factors in a work of art (which yet may exist there in spite of our incapacity), we shall cease caring for it the moment we are tired of the phase of life or thought or feeling which it embodies.

BERNARD BERENSON

(62)

The problem for the artist is almost always the same, namely, that of discovering a possible synthesis for life and form. Sometimes life itself seems to have attained to form, as in the case of those lizards which modern Italian craftsmen convert directly into bronze by purely mechanical means. But the form then has only the trivial expressiveness implied in the unfamiliarity of a change of material from living tissue to rigid bronze. This undoubtedly gives the mind a slight stimulus whereby we contemplate more tranquilly the actual form, than when we chance upon the living creature. At the other end of the scale are the innumerable stylisations of animal form which those too impatiently æsthetic Egyptians practised. Here nearly always we find the life crushed out in the process of a too rigid, too " decorative " formula.

Somewhere in between will be, I think, all the greatest works of art.

ROGER FRY

(63)

We must never forget that the emotion which the painter has to cultivate is not the emotion of the poet, the musician, or the archæologist, but the emotion that is stirred by the pictorial aspect of things and by that aspect alone.

Whatever charm his subject may have for him by reason of its association with life or literature, he will make a bad picture of it if he allows this charm to come between him and the thought of its pictorial aspect.   C. J. HOLMES

(64)

NORWICH, *January* 1816

. . . In your letter you wish me to give you my opinion of your picture. I should have liked it better if you had made it more of a whole. . . . Breadth must be attended to ; if you paint but a muscle, give it Breadth. Your doing the same by the sky, making parts broad and of a good shape, that they may come in with your composition, forming one grand plan of light and shade, this must always please a good eye, and keep the attention of the spectator, and give delight to every one. Trifles in nature must be overlooked, that we may have our feelings raised by seeing the whole picture at a glance, not knowing how or why we are so charmed. I have written you a long rigmarole story about giving dignity to whatever you paint. . . .   JOHN CROME ("Old Crome")

(65)

Every work of art which one enjoys with complete æsthetic apprehension becomes, for the time being, the spirit's universe. No conscious reference to anything outside the work of art is relevant ; we are absorbed and englobed within it. But in the interior of a great building this spiritual isolation is happily symbolised and, as it were, incarnated by our being physically shut off from all other life. It is as though when one looked at a picture one could enter into its space corporally as well as ideally.

And so, in a great interior, mere spatial extension, which is the most universal and therefore the most unnoticed condition of our physical existence, suddenly becomes a matter of profound importance and of the richest spiritual significance. Some absolute quantity of extension is necessary since we have a body of determinate size ; but beyond that, mere vastness of absolute scale is only impressive in a superficial way. We feel we are being unfairly used if that mere vastness is not illumined by the significance of harmonious relations. It is the manner in which the ideated movements in different directions are stimulated in the spirit that counts, and how these movements are checked by the limiting surfaces : whether, for instance, they are brought to a sudden abrupt close by a flat impenetrable wall or gradually deflected by a curved surface, or, as it were, enfolded in the shell of a dome, or united to possible prolongations by an archway or an arcade, or more subtly united and more gently checked by the intricacies of light and shade on a plastically modelled surface. It is by the infinite possibilities of interplay of such and similar motives that the architect creates the total impression of an interior. On the outside of a building he is modelling in the round, like a sculptor ; within he is

shaping the concavity of a space, which is none the less ideal in its effect upon the spirit for being actually constructed. He is working here on lines more familiar to the painter, whose aim Seurat summed up as being " creuser une toile "—" to hollow space out of a flat canvas."
                                                                            ROGER FRY

(66)

But what is this unheard-of art of space-composition ? To begin with, it is not at all a synonym for " composition " as ordinarily used, a word by which, I take it, we mean such an arrangement of objects within a given area as will satisfy our feelings for symmetry, harmony, compactness, and clearness. But all this arrangement is with reference to a flat surface, and extensions up and down, to right and left of an ideal centre—not inwards. . . . Now space-composition differs from ordinary composition in the first place most obviously in that it is not an arrangement to be judged as extending only laterally, or up and down on a flat surface, but as extending inwards in depth as well. It is composition in three dimensions, and not in two ; in the cube, not merely on the surface. And, though less obviously, space-composition differs even more widely from ordinary composition in its effects. The latter, reduced to its elements, plays only on our feeling for pattern—itself a compound of direct optical sensations and their mental consequences, of faint impressions of balance, and fainter ideated movements. Space-composition is much more potent. Producing as it does immediate effects—how and why cannot here be discussed—on the vasomotor system, with every change of space we suffer on the instant a change in our circulation and our breathing—a change which we become aware of as a feeling of heightened or lowered vitality. . . . Hence the likeness so often felt, but, to my knowledge at least, never explained, between music and architecture— the latter, in so far as it is not merely superior carpentry, being essentially a manifestation, the most specific and the most powerful, of the art of space-composition.

With this last sentence many will agree who then will wonder how in painting space-composition can have a place, unless, indeed, it reproduce architecture. But a painting that represents architecture is intrinsically no more of a space-composition than any other picture. This art comes into existence only when we get a sense of space, not as a void, as something merely negative, such as we customarily have, but, on the contrary, as something very positive and definite, able to confirm our consciousness of being, to heighten our feeling of vitality . . . as transporting, as exalting as are those things only which build up the ideal life. Near as it is to music in the form of great architecture, space-composition is even more musical in painting ; for here there is less of the tyranny of mere masses of material, and their inexorable suggestions of weight and support ; here there is more freedom, less is determined for one, although nothing is left to wayward fancy ; and here, with this seeming greater freedom, many more instruments are playing to woo us away from our tight, painfully limited selves, and to dissolve us into the space presented, until at last we seem to become its indwelling, permeating spirit.
                                                                    BERNARD BERENSON

(67)

One chief aspect of order in a work of art is unity ; unity of some kind is necessary for our restful contemplation of the work of art as a whole, since if it lacks unity we cannot contemplate it in its entirety, but we shall pass outside it to other things necessary to complete its unity.

In a picture this unity is due to a balancing of the attractions to the eye about the central line of the picture. The result of this balance of attractions is that the eye rests willingly within the bounds of the picture. Dr. Denman Ross of Harvard University has made a most valuable study of the elementary considerations upon which this balance is based in his *Theory of Pure Design*. He sums up his results in the formula that a composition is of value in proportion to the number of orderly connections which it displays.

Dr. Ross wisely restricts himself to the study of abstract and meaningless forms. The moment representation is introduced, forms have an entirely new set of values. Thus a line which indicated the sudden bend of a head in a certain direction would have far more than its mere value as line in the composition because of the attraction which a marked gesture has for the eye. In almost all paintings this disturbance of the purely decorative values by reason of the representative effect takes place, and the problem becomes too complex for geometrical proof.

This merely decorative unity is, moreover, of very different degrees of intensity in different artists and in different periods. The necessity for a closely woven geometrical texture in the composition is much greater in heroic and monumental design than in genre pieces on a small scale.

It seems also probable that our appreciation of unity in pictorial design is of two kinds. We are so accustomed to consider only the unity which results from the balance of a number of attractions presented to the eye simultaneously in a framed picture that we forget the possibility of other pictorial forms.

In certain Chinese paintings the length is so great that we cannot take in the whole picture at once, nor are we intended to do so. Sometimes a landscape is painted upon a roll of silk so long that we can only look at it in successive segments. As we unroll it at one end and roll it up at the other, we traverse wide stretches of country, tracing, perhaps, all the vicissitudes of a river from its source to the sea, and yet, when this is well done, we have received a very keen impression of pictorial unity.

Such a successive unity is, of course, familiar to us in literature and music, and it plays its part in the graphic arts. It depends upon the forms being presented to us in such a sequence that each successive element is felt to have a fundamental and harmonious relation with that which preceded it. I suggest that in looking at drawings our sense of pictorial unity is largely of this nature; we feel, if the drawing be a good one, that each modulation of the line as our eye passes along it gives order and variety to our sensations. Such a drawing may be almost entirely lacking in the geometrical balance which we are accustomed to demand in paintings, and yet have, in a remarkable degree, unity.

ROGER FRY

(68)

Rhythm is a constraint; it produces an unconquerable desire to yield, to join in; not only the step of the foot, but also the soul itself follows the measure—probably the souls of the gods also, as people thought. . . .

Looked at and investigated as a whole, was there anything *more serviceable* to the ancient superstitious species of human being than rhythm ? People could do anything with it : they could make labour go on magically ; they could compel a god to appear, to be near at hand, and to listen to them ; they could arrange the future for themselves according to their will ; they could unburden the soul of any kind of excess (of anxiety, of mania, of sympathy, of revenge), and not only their own soul, but the souls of the most evil spirits—without verse a person was nothing, by means of verse a person became almost a god. Such a fundamental feeling no longer allows itself to be fully eradicated, and even now, after millenniums of long labour in combating such superstition, the wisest of us occasionally becomes the fool of rhythm, be it only that one *perceives* a thought to be *truer* when it has a metrical form and approaches with a divine hopping.

NIETZSCHE

(69)

But what is rhythm ? No one seems to know precisely, though we can often recognise what we cannot define.

Rhythm has been limited, as a technical term, to sound in music and speech ; but we are probably nearer its essence when we speak of the rhythmical movements of the body, as in games or the dance. We all know, by experience, that in order to apply the energy of the body to the utmost effect, we must discover a certain related order of movements ; and when this is found and followed, a power comes into play which far surpasses in effect the application of brute strength and muscular effort. We rightly recognise this order of movements as rhythm. It is not a mere mechanical succession of beats and intervals. Well, in every kind of art is it not just such a discovered principle in ourselves which is of the essence of the impulse towards creation ? It is a spiritual rhythm passing into and acting on material things.

I would suggest that the most typical, as it is probably the oldest of the arts, is the Dance ; not the dance of modern Europe, but the dance of old Greece, old China, old Japan . . . and I suppose that in all countries, among primitive peoples, the dance has had a religious character, as if, in the abandonment and passion of movement, the intense and glowing realisation of conscious life, might be recovered a spark of the divine ecstasy of creation whence issued the " dancing stars " and the " dædal earth." An Indian text says of Siva, the Destroyer and Preserver, that he is the dancer who, like the heat latent in firewood, diffuses his power on mind and matter and makes them dance in their turn.

In the dance, as so understood, there is the germ of music, of drama, and, in a sense, of sculpture and painting too. Even in architecture there is an essential analogy. For the walls, the roof, the pillars of a great cathedral are in the mind of the architect no mere mass of stones, but so many co-ordinated energies, each exerting force in relation to each other, like the tense limbs of a body possessed by a single mood of rapt exaltation. In the dance the body becomes a work of art, a plastic idea, infinitely expressive of emotion and of thought ; and in every art the material taken up, just so far as the artist is successful, is merged into idea.

Sculpture and painting are not, it is true, capable of actual movement, but they suggest movement. Every statue, every picture, is a series of ordered relations, controlled, as the body is controlled in the dance, by the will to express a single idea. A study of the most rudimentary abstract design will show that the units of line and mass are in reality energies capable of acting on each other ; and, if we discover a way to put these energies into rhythmic relation, the design at once becomes animated, our imagination enters into it ; our minds are brought into rhythmic relation with the design, which has become charged with the capability of movement and of life. In a bad painting the units of form, mass, colour, are robbed of their potential energy, isolated, because brought into no organic relationship, they do not work together and therefore none of them has a tithe even of its own effect. It is just so with the muscular movements of a bad player at a game, or bad dancer.

When the rhythm is found we feel that we are put into touch with life, not only our own life, but the life of the whole world. It is as if we moved to the music which set the stars in motion. . . .

It is not . . . in painting . . . a question of line and colour only. To attempt to make an abstraction of these qualities is a fatal mistake ; it cannot in reality be done. The power of rhythm is such that not only sounds and forms and colours, but the meanings associated with them become different, take on a new life, or rather yield up their full potentiality of life, fused into radiance and warmth by an inner fire. Perhaps no people has ever been stirred by a great idea until that idea was animated and made memorable by finding its right expression in rhythmical phrase.   LAURENCE BINYON

(70)

The measure flows, as it were, unconsciously from the mood of the poet. If he thought about it while writing the poem, he would go mad, and produce nothing of value.

There is a charm in rhythm. It makes us believe that its grandeur is part of our own being.   GOETHE

(71)

And first from the *origin* of metre. This I would trace to the balance in the mind effected by that spontaneous effort which strives to hold in check the workings of passion. . . .

Metre in itself is simply a stimulant of the attention, and thereby excites the question : " Why is the attention to be thus stimulated ? " Now the question cannot be answered by the pleasure of the metre itself : for this we have shown to be *conditional*, and dependent on the appropriateness of the thoughts and expressions to which the metrical form is superadded. . . .

Metre . . . having been connected with *poetry*, most often and by a peculiar fitness, whatever else is combined with *metre*, though itself not *essentially* poetic, must have nevertheless some property in common with poetry, as an intermedium of affinity, a sort (if I may dare borrow a well-known phrase from technical chemistry) of *mordaunt* between it and the superadded metre. Now poetry, Mr. Wordsworth truly affirms, does always imply PASSION: which word must be here understood, in its general sense, as an excited state of the feelings and faculties. And as every passion has its proper pulse, so will it likewise have its characteristic modes of expression.   COLERIDGE

(72)

The common explanation of the love of the metrical charm is, I believe, the love of patterns. . . .

All artistic beauty exhibits a mastery, a triumph of grace; and this implies a difficulty overcome—for no mastery or grace can appear in the doing of whatever you suppose any man could do with equal ease if he chose. And since in a perfect work (music, perhaps, provides the best examples), all difficulty is so mastered that it entirely disappears and would not be thence inferred, it is necessary that for general appreciation there should be some recognition or consciousness of the formal conditions in which the difficulty is implicit. And thus one of the uses of second-rate works of art is that they reveal and remind us of the material obstacles. . . .

. . . A great deal of our pleasure in beauty, whether natural or artistic, depends on slight variations of a definite form. Fancy if all roses were as triangular in shape as all equilateral triangles! The fundamental motive of this pleasure may be described as a balance between the expected and the unexpected—the expected being a sedative soothing lulling principle, and the unexpected a stimulated awakening principle. Too much of the type would be tedious, too much of the unexpected would worry. The unexpected stimulates the consciousness, but you must also be conscious of the type, or this *balance* may be regarded as a *strife* between two things, the fixed type and the freedom of the variations.   ROBERT BRIDGES

(73)

The truth is really this: content and form must be clearly distinguished in art, but must not be separately qualified as artistic, precisely because their relation only is artistic —that is their unity, understood not as an abstract, dead unity, but as concrete and living, which is that of the synthesis *a priori*; and art is a true *æsthetic synthesis a priori* of feeling and image in the intuition, as to which it may be repeated that feeling without image is blind, and image without feeling is void. Feeling and image do not exist for the artistic spirit outside the synthesis; they may have existence from another point of view in another plane of knowledge, and feeling will then be the practical aspect of the spirit that loves and hates, desires and dislikes, and the image will be the inanimate residue of art, the withered leaf, prey of the wind of imagination and of amusement's caprice. All this has no concern with the artist or the æsthetician: for art is no vain imagining or tumultuous passionality, but the surpassing of this act by means of another act, or, if it be preferred, the substitution for this tumult of another's tumult, that of the longing to create and to contemplate with the joy and the anguish of artistic creation. It is therefore indifferent, or merely a question of terminological opportuneness, whether we should present art as content or as form, provided that it be always recognised that the content is formed and the form filled, that feeling is figured feeling and the figure a figure that is felt. . . . Feeling, or state of the soul, is not a particular content, but the whole universe seen *sub specie intuitionis.* . . .

Another not less fallacious distinction (to which the words " content " and " form " are also applied) separates *intuition* from *expression,* the image from the physical transla- tion of the image. It places on the one side phantasms of feelings, images of men, of animals, of landscapes, of actions, of adventures, and so on ; and on the other sounds, tones, lines, colours, and so on ; calling the first the external, the second the internal element of art : the one *art,* properly so called, the other *technique.* . . . What has here been distinguished cannot be united because it has been badly distinguished ; how can something external and extraneous to the internal become united to the internal and express it ?

CROCE

(74)

Professors of literature have an idea that in art there is substance and form, the vessel and that which the vessel contains, and, possessing the vessel, that one may then do what one likes with the liquid. What contains and what is contained are inseparable ; they are born and grow together as veins and arteries and the blood which they hold. The blood, apart from the vessels, and the vessels, emptied of their blood, are equally dead things. A physiologist must understand anatomy ; but nothing is more dangerous for him or for his clients than that he should reason as an anatomist. The analysis of litera- ture is a similar study ; when one works upon the living thing, it is necessary to reunite the elements which the analysis has separated, and convince oneself that to think well and to write well is one and the same movement, a movement which sets in motion two jointly and severally answerable activities.

RÉMY DE GOURMONT

(75)

Leibnitz . . . considered only its (music's) immediate external significance, its form. But if it were nothing more, the satisfaction which it affords would be like that which we feel when a sum in arithmetic comes out right, and could not be that intense pleasure with which we see the deepest recesses of our nature find utterance. From our standpoint, therefore, at which the æsthetic effect is the criterion, we must attribute to music a far more serious and deep significance, connected with the inmost nature of the world and our own self, and in reference to which the arithmetical proportions to which it may be reduced are related, not as the thing signified, but merely as the sign. That in some sense music must be related to the world as the representation to the thing represented, as the copy to the original, we may conclude from the analogy of the other arts, all of which possess this character, and affect us on the whole in the same way as it does. . . . Further its representative relation to the universe must be very deep, absolutely true, and strikingly accurate, yet—very obscure. . . .

SCHOPENHAUER

(76)

Is there any art in which the form does not follow the idea in this intimate way ? In painting, in poetry, *the form is one with the conception.*   DELACROIX

(77)

There are no beautiful thoughts without beautiful forms, and conversely. As it is impossible to extract from a physical body the qualities which really constitute it—colour, extension, and the like—without reducing it to a hollow abstraction—in a word, without destroying it—just so is it impossible to detach the form from the idea, for the idea only exists by virtue of the form. FLAUBERT

(78)

The idea which puts the form together cannot itself be the form. It is above form and is its essence.

Remember there is a difference between form as proceeding and shape as super-induced; the latter is either the death or the imprisonment of the thing; the former is the self-witnessing and self-effected sphere of agency. COLERIDGE

(79)

The human body is not the dress or apparel of the human spirit; far more mysterious is the mode of their union. Call the two elements A and B; then it is impossible to point out A as existing aloof from B, or *vice versa*. A exists in and through B; B exists in and through A. . . . Imagery is sometimes not the mere alien apparelling of a thought, and of the nature to be detached from the thought, but is the coefficient that, being super-added to something else, absolutely *makes* the thought as a third and separate existence. DE QUINCEY

(80)

This is an excellent opportunity to establish a rational and historic theory of beauty, in opposition to the theory of an absolute and unique beauty; to show that beauty is always and inevitably of a double nature, although it may give the impression of a nature that is single; for the difficulty of realising the variable elements of beauty in the unity of the impression does nothing to lessen the necessity of variety in its composition. Beauty is composed of an eternal and invariable element, the quality of which is very difficult to determine, and of a relative and incidental element which may be, whether consecutively or simultaneously, epoch, vogue, moral, or passion. Without this second element, which is like the amusing, stimulating, appetising outside of the divine sweet-meat, the first element would be indigestible, unadaptable, and unsuitable to human nature. I defy anyone to find any sample whatsoever of beauty which does not contain the two elements. . . .

The duality of art is the fatal consequence of the duality of man. You can consider, if you like, the eternal part as the soul of art, and the variable element as its body. . . .

I have more than once explained these things; these words will be clear enough to those who love the play of abstract thought; but I know that French readers, for the most part, will understand little, and I hate myself to discuss the positive and real part of my subject. BAUDELAIRE

(81)

A poet participates in the eternal, the infinite, and the one ; as far as relates to his conceptions, time and space and number are not—a poet considers the vices of his contemporaries as the temporary dress in which his creations must be arrayed and which cover without concealing the eternal proportions of their beauty. An epic or dramatic personage is understood to wear theirs around his soul, as he may the ancient armour or modern uniform around his body. The beauty of the internal nature cannot be so far concealed by its accidental vesture, but that the spirit of its form shall communicate itself to the very disguise and indicate the shape it hides from the manner in which it is worn. . . . Few poets of the highest class have chosen to exhibit the beauty of their conceptions in its native truth and splendour ; and it is doubtful whether the alloy of costume, habit, etc., be not necessary to temper this planetary music for mortal ears.

SHELLEY

(82)

A true work of art, like a true work of nature, never ceases to open boundlessly before the mind. We examine,—we are impressed with it,—it produces its effect ; but it can never be all comprehended, still less can its essence, its value, be expressed in words. . . .

We can hardly speak adequately of a high work of art without also speaking of art in general ; since all art is comprehended in it and each one is able, according to his powers, to develop the universal out of such a special case. . . .

. . . Art has many steps, in all of which there have been admirable artists ; but a perfect work of art embraces all the qualities that are elsewhere encountered only separately.

GOETHE

(83)

It remains now to derive from Form the function of art :[1] to consider what is meant by artistic significance and what artistic unity has to do with it. The answer to all such questions is implied in the profoundest aphorism ever contributed to the theory of art—Bacon's assertion that in poetry we have " the shows of things submitted to the desire of the mind " ; the exposition of this will make it applicable to any art.

What is the central, the inveterate desire of the mind, which all man's practical and spiritual activities imply ? It is the desire for significant experience, the desire to be living in, and a conscious part of, a significant world. Not that we desire to know what the world means ; in one sense we know that already, and in another sense we can never know it ; the world can only *mean* itself, a proposition in which the most of us take but faint interest. But a significant world is a world in which nothing happens out of relation with the whole of things, in which everything must perfectly cohere with the rest and nothing can occur

[1] By the function of art I mean its peculiar relation with the rest of life. Our instinctive belief, that art must have a function, is due to that sovereign idea of the coherence of things which finds its most unequivocal assertion in art itself, as we are now to see. But though we can derive from form the nature of the function of art, the possibility of a function at all (*i.e.* of having an effective relation with life in general) is clearly given by the fact that art is communication.

irrelevantly : a world in which each is for all and all is for each. That is the world we desire ; and that is the world we never quite get—*except in art*. Whatever we experience in art, we experience in a perfectly coherent and orderly manner, in a necessary and intricate interrelationship with the rest of our experience there : in, that is to say, a significant manner. For what was said of a significant *world* will apply to *things*. What do we intend by the " significance " of a thing ? Is it " what the thing means " ? But " what the thing means " can only be what is implied by the thing in terms of other things. So that significance really is relationship, the degree in which experience involves and implies other experiences. A thing is said to be significant when its reference to other things is unmistakable ; and the richer the reference, the greater the significance. But in a work of art, everything refers to and implies everything else in it ; all is interrelation and coherence ; and every part is manifestly owned by the whole, and the whole is intended by every part. So that in art the impression of every fractional or momentary detail is an impression of the significance of things, and the impression of the whole work is an impression of a significant world. Chance or irrelevance can have no place in art ; and chance is the enemy of significance, since it is an intrusion of irrelevance, a lapse from coherence. It is the incoherent, the irrelevant, which we are continually trying to eliminate from our practical or intellectual or other experience. . . .

And so, in general, whatever art gives us is given as an instance of a world of unquestioned order, measure, government ; a world in which experience occurs with perfect security, knowing that the firm interrelationship of its process can never be dislocated by chance—the world which is " the desire of the mind." And it is experience of *this* world which is so presented : " the *shows* of things "—æsthetic experience.

Now we see why Form is the chief excellence of art. It is because art presents its matter as Form that it effects this profoundly desirable impression of coherence, of interrelationship, and so of significance both of parts and of whole. For it is by Form that the matter, whatever it be, is accepted as a unity ; and Form is not, as we have seen, a boundary imposed on the matter from without, not even a final fastening together of matter already tolerably shaped, as a tyre binds the felloes of a wheel ; Form as the expression of ultimate unity is inherent through all the matter of a work of art, and is constantly working through every detail of expression towards its completion : artistic expression, indeed, merely has to complete itself in order to achieve its most important aspect, *Form*. It can only be, then, that the impression of unity in a work of art is an impression of thoroughly organic unity ; it is nothing but the total impression of matter which has been throughout presented as necessarily interrelated, whether the process of arriving at this total impression has worked in space (as with painting and architecture) or in time (as with poetry and music). It is by virtue of its Form, therefore, that a work of art gives us that perfectly coherent and mutually dependent experience which has the quality we call significance. And by virtue of its Form, the presentation of even tragical matter, which would elsewhere be unendurably distressing, can in art be supremely satisfying and severely exhilarating : as in " Othello " or " Antigone," Mantegna's " Dead Christ " or Michelangelo's " Dawn."

In art even sorrowful matter is presented as belonging to a region of experience

4

where nothing can be incoherent or irrelevant, where everything that happens is known to be necessary for the completion of existence. Even that which horrifies in actual life becomes in art an instance of the significance we desire of things . . . satisfaction . . . at seeing the stuff of the world we know too well becoming an establisht image of the world of profound and inevitable significance : in a word, of the ideal world.

LASCELLES ABERCROMBIE

(84)

The writers who, we say, are for all time or are simply good, and who intoxicate us, have one common and very important characteristic : they are all going towards something and are summoning you towards it too, and you feel, not with your mind but with your whole being, that they have some object. . . . The best of them are realistic and paint life as it is, but through every line's being soaked in the consciousness of an object, you feel, besides life as it is, the life which ought to be, and that captivates you. . . .

CHEHOV (TCHEKHOV)

(85)

Poesy . . . commonly exceeds the measure of nature, joining at pleasure things which in nature would never have come together, and introducing things which in nature would never have come to pass ; just as painting likewise does. This is the work of the imagination.

For as the sensible world is inferior in dignity to the rational soul, Poesy seems to bestow upon human nature those things which history denies to it ; and to satisfy the mind with the shadows of things when the substance cannot be obtained. For if the matter be attentively considered, a sound argument may be drawn from Poesy, to show that there is agreeable to the spirit of man a more ample greatness, a more perfect order, and a more beautiful variety than it can anywhere (since the Fall) find in nature.

And therefore (Poesy) was even thought to have some participation of divineness, because it doth raise and erect the mind by submitting the shows of things to the desires of the mind ; whereas reason doth buckle and bow the mind unto the nature of things.

BACON

(86)

Heaven borne, the soul a heavenward course must hold ;
Beyond the visible world she soars to seek
(For what delights the sense is false and weak) [1]
Ideal form, the universal mould.
The wise man, I affirm, can find no rest
In that which perishes ; nor will he lend
His heart to aught which doth on time depend,
That kills the soul. . . .   MICHAEL ANGELO BUONARROTI

[1] If what delights the sense is false and weak, an important element in the art of Michael Angelo and all other artists would be discredited.

(87)

I agree with Schopenhauer, that one of the most powerful motives that attract people to science and art is the longing to escape from everyday life with its painful coarseness and desolating bareness, and to break the fetters of our ever-changing desires. It impels those of keener sensibility out of their personal existence into the world of objective perception and understanding. It is a motive force of like kind to that which drives the dweller in noisy confused cities to restful Alpine heights whence he seems to have an outlook on eternity : associated with this negative motive is the positive motive which impels men to seek a simplified synoptic view of the world conformable to their own nature, overcoming the world by replacing it with this picture. The painter, the poet, the philosopher, the scientist, all do this each in his own way.   EINSTEIN

(88)

Poetry defeats the curse which binds us to be subjected to the accident of surrounding impressions. . . . It creates for us a being within our being. It makes us the inhabitant of a world to which the familiar world is a chaos.

Poetry redeems from decay the visitations of the divinity in man.

Poetry turns all things to loveliness ; it exalts the beauty of that which is most beautiful and it adds beauty to that which is deformed. It marries exaltation and horror ; grief and pleasure ; eternity and change : it subdues to union, under its light yoke, all irreconcilable things.   SHELLEY

(89)

It was . . . when my mind was in a state of perfect composure and free from external distraction, that I first obtained some idea of your Grand Master (Sebastian Bach). I said to myself, it is as if the eternal harmony were conversing with itself, as it may have done, in the bosom of God, just before the creation of the world. So likewise did it move in my inmost soul, and it seemed as if I neither possessed nor needed ears, nor any other sense—least of all the eyes.   GOETHE *to* ZELTER

(90)

It is my temper, and I like it the better, to affect all harmony ; . . . For there is a musick wherever there is a harmony, order, or proportion ; and this far we may maintain the music of the spheres ; for these well-ordered motions and regular paces, though they give no sound unto the ear, yet to the understanding they strike a note most full of harmony. . . . (Music) is an hieroglyphical and shadowed lesson of the whole world and creatures of God—such a melody to the ear as the whole world, well understood, would afford the understanding. In brief, it is a sensible fit of that harmony which intellectually sounds in the ears of God. It unties the ligaments of my frame, takes me to pieces, dilates me out of myself, and by degrees, methinks, resolves me into heaven.   SIR THOMAS BROWNE

(91)

To accomplish a mystical disintegration is not the function of any art ; if any art seems to accomplish it, the effect is only incidental, being involved, perhaps, in the process of constructing the proper object of that art, as we might cut down trees, and dig them up by the roots to lay the foundations of a temple. For every art looks to the building up of something. And just because the image of the world built up by common sense and natural science is an inadequate image (a skeleton, which needs the filling of sensation before it can live), therefore the moment when we realise its inadequacy is the moment when the higher arts find their opportunity. When the world is shattered to bits they can come and " build it nearer to the heart's desire."

The great function of poetry is precisely this : to repair to the material of experience, seizing hold of the reality of sensation and fancy beneath the surface of conventional ideas, and then, out of that living but indefinite material, to build new structures, richer, finer, fitter to the primary tendencies of our nature, truer to the ultimate possibilities of the soul. Our descent into the elements of our being is then justified by our subsequent freer ascent toward its goal ; we revert to sense only to find food for reason ; we destroy conventions only to construct ideals.   GEORGE SANTAYANA

COMMENTARY

In Figs. 79–84 are works of art which illustrate Ruskin's remarks on p. 36. Fig. 79 gives us " art without facts," in a fine piece of savage embroidery. Fig. 81, although a water-colour, might well be a photograph. It shows no trace of effort to arrange and harmonise the natural forms in the ordered sequence of design, and can well be described as " facts without art." Fig. 80 gives us " art and facts " in a beautiful example of mediæval sculpture, where the geometric nature of the design is clearly marked. In Figs. 82–84 " art and facts " are again manifest, although in more subtle forms. Owing to the miraculous power of design, still life, in the hands of a great master, can become a vehicle for profound sensuous and spiritual experience. In Fig. 82 we find pleasure in the quality and texture of the painting, in the light and shadow, in the bloom and colour of the fruit, and in the substance and surface of the cup and bowl. But we also find a deeper delight. We feel that the artist, using the elemental and underlying forms of cylinder, sphere, and hemisphere as the basis of his design, has erected a structure that is mysterious and yet stable, where the imagination rests, living intensely and yet at peace. To this illustration the reader should return again and again, continually comparing it with the still life illustrated above. A great painting will only yield its secret slowly.[1]

Design such as this is subtle and irregular in contrast with the more geometric type in Fig. 84. Here the majesty and beauty of the Christian scene is expressed with the directness and austerity of a monument. Fig. 83 is a particularly good example of irregular design. Through tenderness of fancy, through delicacy of texture, through sensuousness restrained and refined, we are conscious of a completely satisfying balance of suggested mass in space. Something fundamental in us responds to the sense of harmony and equilibrium communicated. Even if a mathematical basis eventually be found to underlie designs such as these, our pleasure in them will always exist without any such conscious reinforcement. Where the nature of design is not fully understood, the term is incorrectly limited to an obviously geometric arrangement of highly conventionalised forms.

[1] This picture should also be studied in connection with the question of the importance of subject-matter in art (see pp. 53–55). The following lines by Schopenhauer might also be considered : " If the . . . subject " (Schopenhauer here refers to the creative artist) " be in a receptive mood, almost every object now falling within its apperception will begin to speak to it, *i.e.* to create in it a vivid, penetrating, and original thought. Hence at times the aspect of an unimportant object or event has become the germ of a great and beautiful work." Or Baudelaire : " In certain almost supernatural states of the soul, the depths of life reveal themselves completely in anything that may happen to meet the eye, no matter how commonplace such a sight may be. It becomes the symbol."

In the series of illustrations 85–95 are works which range from an example of " art without facts "
to a work of art charged with profound psychological meaning. Yet in no instance does the experience
overlap the form. In each case the subject-matter has been conceived in terms of form and arrangement of form, and the descriptive element never predominates over pictorial considerations. Great
art cannot be measured scientifically : it can only be gauged by the richness, quality, and precision
of its experience as conceived and communicated in terms of design. Both Figs. 85 and 95 reproduce
experiences perfectly expressed and communicated. But the experience crystallised in the first illustration is obviously of a much simpler order.[1]

In Fig. 85 the problem faced has been that of adapting purely geometric pattern to the bodily forms
to be decorated. In Fig. 86 the forms of the Maya numerals are almost, but not completely, reduced
to abstract terms. Human heads are discernible, and forms reminiscent of flowers, foliage, and plum-
age. In both designs we see elementary units of mass and line animated by the manner in which
they are related (see p. 44). When we look at the capital of a column, illustrated in Fig. 87, our first
impression is probably one of pleasure at the beauty of the design. It is only when we look more
closely that we realise the very unpleasant subject-matter, namely, vultures devouring a corpse. Fig. 88
shows a similar preoccupation with formal, rather than descriptive, elements. The Romanesque sculptor
does not appear to have given a thought to the psychological interest of his subject. The same
intense interest in formal significance is apparent in the next three illustrations. The Chinese painter
(Fig. 89) has not attempted to earn our admiration by a realistic representation of the appearance of nature. His mind is set on beauty of a more profound and permanent order. In the same
way, the Cretan artist of the High Renaissance (Fig. 91) submits the interest of his story to the fiery
rhythms of his mind, and in his art finds the order and peace that he lacked in life, the charmed repose
of which Mr. Binyon speaks on p. 13. As we contemplate the portrait Fig. 90, we are stilled with
its calm. Here we find the solid unity into which the heat of a profound experience has cooled and
set. In Fig. 92 we have the type of heroic and monumental design on a grand scale that Mr. Fry
describes on p. 42. The treatment of the wooded landscape in Fig. 93 is so charming, decorative,
and gay, that the sepia drawing takes on the character of a chintz in three dimensions, a classic rendering of a rococo theme. Figs. 94 and 95 show us equally subtle designs, without obvious geometric
basis. More than one hundred and fifty years separate their creations in time, and the dreams of the
Renaissance are divided by a gulf from the visions of the Middle Ages, yet none the less the formal
nature of each conception, and the profound sense of plastic relationships expressed, bridge all divisions
and unite the works. In connection with these last three pictures, reference should be made to Mr.
Fry's remarks on the complexity of design which results when purely decorative values are disturbed
by representative considerations.

While considering the relation of formal to psychological significance, reference must be made
to Fig. B, Plate LI. In all the range of art it would be difficult to find a version of the subject
which so clearly expresses the intensity of the love of the mother for her child, and her sense of fore-
boding at some mystic realisation of what is to befall him. Yet, in spite of this, the picture is far
from popular and presents great difficulty to many minds. The Christ Child seems so ugly that pleasure

---

[1] Those who are interested in the question of how design arises may note that the designs of the Bushongo
tribe, of whose work Fig. 79 is an example, are produced by some form of preconscious reason (see " Central African
Embroideries," Joyce, *Burlington Magazine*, May 1912, p. 91 ; and also *On the Trail of the Bushongo*, Torday (Seeley),
p. 220). Compare also Miss Marion Richardson's method of basing her teaching of drawing upon images of abstract
form derived from the unconscious, and the results obtained by her pupils (see Fig. 28). Henri Poincaré, the
mathematician, has described how he has worked consciously and unsuccessfully at a mathematical problem, and
how, later, the solution has come to his mind, suddenly and spontaneously. From the same unconscious source
would appear to come the artist's largely intuitive power to create an ordered sequence of forms, although it must
be remembered that as the mind of man develops and matures, his work is more fully subjected to his intellectual
and critical activities. The mistake must not be made, however, of believing that all artists work in the same way,
or that psychology has yet explained the creative activity of art.

is impossible. Mr. Roger Fry has suggested that the artist depicted Jesus as a wrinkled newborn child in swaddling clothes to symbolise the bonds of the flesh which Christ took on. Once this suggestion is accepted, annoyance ceases. The spectator has escaped from an inhibition, and is free, for the first time, to see the picture as it is, for the contemplation of art is impossible in an atmosphere of irritation. But with those familiar with art, and sensitive to it, matters are different. Responding readily to design, they find no obstacle in the face of the Christ Child, and no barrier in the formal presentation of the scene, which is plastic rather than illustrative. They realise that in the picture we have that third and separate existence described by De Quincey (p. 47), which is neither content nor form, but the union of both. As in Figs. 39 and 84, we are aware of a sense of something universal rather than of the circumstances of a particular scene. The subject interest is not so much the love of an individual mother for an individual child as love in its essence. Those sensitive to art will find that consciousness of the details of the picture will slowly fade before the general sense of harmony and equilibrium that results from the design, and the feeling of reality that is communicated. The remark of a boy of thirteen might be quoted in conclusion : " I like that picture, because a mother's sympathy is not always told by looks."

As a foil to this picture, a lamentably popular painting of the same subject stands by its side (Fig. A). It is hoped that those who have had the patience to follow these pages will feel that there is not a trace of artistic impulse or formal significance in this compost of melodrama and sentimentality.

The picture of the first Madonna and Child has been discussed at length because it illustrates clearly some of the most difficult problems of art. Leaving these problems, we will now reconsider the question of two- and three-dimensional design to which frequent reference has already been made. It will be found that although most works of art have two-dimensional beauty, and others embody a design that is expressive both from the two- and the three-dimensional aspects, nevertheless one or the other character will be the more clearly marked. The emphasis will lie with the silhouette, or with the relationship of the forms in depth, as described by Mr. Berenson on p. 41.

In Figs. 96–99 we have examples of design where the emphasis is laid on a two-dimensional system. The formal relationships are planned to take effect up and down and across the surface of the panel, wall or material, rather than arranged to suggest volume, the third dimension of depth, and the balance of forms in this depth. This two-dimensional system can give us the effect of breadth as outlined by Crome (p. 40), and very beautiful design can result from its employment. In many instances it is the only suitable system. But when we turn to the vision of St. Eustace (Fig. 100) and compare it with the hunting scene below (Fig. 101), the contrast between the two systems is striking.[1]

The first hunting scene is full of charming fancy. The line is sensitive and animated, each unit has firmness, delicacy, and precision, but there is little suggestion of depth. The forms are largely two-dimensional, and are not united into any very definite and harmonious structure. They are scattered up and down the picture with descriptive rather than formal intention, as so often in pictures inspired by the Northern tradition. But when we turn to the second hunting scene we feel the contrast between design in two dimensions and design in three, and also between an arrangement of the parts that is unsatisfactory and one that splendidly succeeds. We become conscious of the third dimension of depth extending behind the surface of the picture plane, a suggested space in which the objects painted take their place in rhythmic disposition. This power of suggesting volume by the recession of planes is shared by all the greatest painters of the West and by many of the East.

The next point to consider more fully in connection with design is the question of subject. Since the beauty of nature and the beauty of art are different things, and since the beauty of art is inseparable from the beauty of design, it follows that the beauty of art is not dependent upon beautiful subject-matter. When we look at Figs. 102 and 103 we cannot say that the statue of the Greek girl is more beautiful than that of the Indian god merely because the dancer is herself beautiful and the god repellent. Both statues have artistic beauty, because both are fine designs. The longer we look at

[1] That Pisanello could successfully place a single form within given limits is clear in Fig. 98.

them the more conscious we become of rhythmic vitality, of a controlled and ordered sequence of movements, of thrusts and counter-thrusts held in balance. It is interesting to examine the means by which the artists have achieved their aims. Take, for example, the arms. Those of the Greek dancer have been thickened in order that the backward thrusts of head and skirts should be counterbalanced by responding weights. The upper arms have become as broad as the face. The problem in the case of the god has been greater, for his four arms, symbolising superhuman prowess, had to be brought into the design. The difficulty has been met by broadening one arm and making it spring from the centre of the back, while grouping the other somewhat lighter arms at an opposite point, thus establishing the balance.[1]

When we turn to Figs. 104 and 105 we are faced by a similar contrast. Which scene in the stable is the work of art ? From the point of natural beauty no one can be expected to prefer the flayed ox. To most people such a sight is repellent with all its associations of butchery. But when the scene flashed across the vision of a great artist, it was not so much the carcass of an ox that he saw, but harmonies of light and shade in which the creature's body was but one of the formal elements in an equilibrium of mass and space. Only a very great artist could be inspired by such a scene and could translate it into the language of great art. The contrasted reproduction is little more than a pleasant illustration. We find no formal significance, no balance of units of light and shade.

In Fig. 106 we have another method of treating unpleasant or unromantic subject-matter. In this case the painter has materialised a mental image of a chair against a background of red tiles. If we object that no floor or chair ever ran uphill we are making a scientific, not an artistic, criticism. The artist must materalise his own vision, and in this picture the formal harmony carries with it its own justification. It is not a case of wilful distortion, painting from a negative, rather than from a positive impulse. It is something seen and felt in an unusual way. As a last test of artistic sensibility, let us turn to Fig. 107. Here we have a painting of Andromeda. As illustration it is valueless. Nothing could be less Greek, nothing more plebeian, than the heroine. No woman could be more destitute of natural beauty or feminine charm. But the beauty of art is there. Its author has envisaged the scene, much as he did the flayed ox, in terms of balanced light and shade, depth and breadth. At all times, in all countries, the artist's real subject-matter is design, in spite of what he himself may believe. What design incorporates can only be of secondary interest ; beautiful women or ugly, apples, roses, meadows, the Holy Family or the slaughter-house ; all can be, in the words of Mr. Roger Fry, the springboard for the artist's leap into infinity. The passage from Schiller (p. 18) can well be re-read at this point.

Another aspect of design, which also presents difficulty to many people, is the question of the relation of beauty to utility, in what are called the lesser or applied arts. Members of arts and crafts societies often hug the belief that everything made by hand, with joy, to serve some useful end, must be beautiful with the beauty of art. This is a pleasant theory, but unfortunately we have only to visit the average arts and crafts exhibition to know that it is not true. More than this, we have only to know the facts, to be familiar with the history of art, to know that it never has been true, even if there ever were joy in this labour that has attempted, but failed, to achieve art. Even in those periods when a fine and vital tradition had raised the whole level of artistic output, counterfeit works were still numerous.

Many writers have held that artistic beauty must be present in any object that performs its function well. In Figs. 108–110 each of the three bowls holds liquid efficiently, while in Fig. 114 each of the two bridges seems admirably adapted to its purpose. Are all the bowls and bridges therefore equally beautiful ? In Fig. 112 the stubby teapot will pour to perfection, and its blunt spout

[1] It may interest the sceptical to know that Rodin, the famous French sculptor, wrote pages of eulogy on the beauty of this statue. The words of Baudelaire may also be remembered : " It is the immense privilege of art that the horrible, artistically expressed, becomes beautiful, and that sorrow, rhymed and cadenced, fills the mind with a ' profound calm.' "

and unprojecting handle are wellnigh unbreakable ; the second teapot is porous, heavy to wield, and has a projecting spout and handle easily broken.   But is the useful teapot the beautiful one ?

Incidentally it may be remarked that the second pot was meant to function well, and looks as if it would.   Our sense of fitness is therefore satisfied and all sides of our mind react pleasantly.   But the beauty of art is an end in itself, something over and above that other type of practical and functional beauty which Plato, and many writers after him, have confused with the beauty of art.

This functional beauty we see in Fig. 116.   The design is beautiful only in so far as it is expressive of speed, power, and perfect adaptation to a given end.   Remove these ideas and no beauty remains.   In contrast see Fig. 117.   Here we find the disinterestedness of art, even if only a minor art.   The search for beauty of design as an end in itself is apparent, and with it the intention to build an efficient state coach.   Fig. 115 shows four different kinds of ornament : a stone vase made to hold a plant ; a stone vase made without practical purpose ; sculptured figures ; and an ornamental scroll.   From the point of view of art each must be judged as form.   Their existence is justified by the experience they hold for sensuous and spiritual contemplation.   If they are unshapely, they have no artistic value whatever practical virtues any of them may have for the utilitarian.   It may be added that the artist who is interested in both aspects of his problem is far more likely to produce a work of art than he who thinks only of beauty of form.   If the idea of utility be divorced in the mind of the craftsman from the idea of form, beauty of form will probably be lost, and objects produced as affected and unpleasing as the vases in Fig. 111.

Finally, since greater realism does not of necessity imply greater art, we cannot say that progress in exact representation is necessarily artistic evolution.   We cannot talk of the evolution of Italian art from Giotto to Giorgione (see Figs. 95 and 94) if we mean by this that the latter was capable of greater powers of accurate representation than the former.   The differences between them are those of temperament, and the changed outlook of their times and traditions of their craft.   But both inhabit the same altitudes.   Similarly, we cannot say of the four Greek heads reproduced in Figs. 118–121 that the last two are greater works of art than the first two because they are more realistic.   We see four ideas expressing themselves in form, and in each case the form is inherent in the idea expressed.   In each we find an imaginative concentration, an ordered disposition and simplification of the planes, a density, and a sensitiveness of texture and handling, which are beauties other than the beauty of the athlete of old Greece.   Each of these heads is beautiful in its own way, similar, yet dissimilar.   We can make our own choice.   The " successive unity " in drawings, described by Mr. Fry on p. 42, can be seen in Figs. 62 and 63.   Many of the quotations in this section of the book must be read a number of times with constant reference to the illustrations before their full import can become clear.

CHAPTER VI

TASTE AND THE APPRECIATION OF ART

ARGUMENT.—*The capacity to enjoy art is inherent in human nature. Some people are endowed with special sensibility, but in others the power has remained latent. But as with other faculties an understanding of art can, as a rule, be stimulated and developed, particularly in the young. Although we can pass almost imperceptibly from one state of mind to another, we cannot both experience and criticise a work of art at the same time. The rational and reflective side of our mind must be in abeyance while the imaginative and contemplative side is at work, and vice versa.*

(92)

Man's desires are limited by his perceptions. None can desire what he has not perceived.

No man can embrace true art until he has explored and cast out false art.

WILLIAM BLAKE

(93)

. . . It is in the nature of all disquisitions on matters of taste, that the reasoner must appeal for his very premises to facts of feeling and of inner sense which all men do not possess, and which many who do possess, and even act upon them, have never reflectively adverted to, and have never made them objects of a full and distinct consciousness. . . . If a man, upon questioning his own experience, can detect no difference *in kind* between the enjoyment derived from the eating of turtle and that from the perception of a new truth : if in *his* feelings a taste *for* Milton is essentially the same as the taste *of* mutton, he may still be a sensible and a valuable member of society ; but it would be a desecration to argue with him on the Fine Arts. . . .

. . . But more especially on the essential difference of the beautiful and the agreeable, rests fundamentally the whole question, which assuredly must possess no vulgar or feeble interest for all who regard the dignity of their own natures : whether the noblest productions of human genius . . . delight us merely by chance, from accidents of local associations—in short, please us because they please us—or whether there exists in the constitution of the human soul a sense, and a regulative principle, which indeed may be stifled and latent in some, and be perverted and denaturalised in others, yet is nevertheless universal, in a given state of intellectual and moral culture ; which is independent of local and temporal circumstances, and dependent only on the degree in which the faculties of the mind are developed ; and which, consequently, it is our duty to cultivate and improve, as soon as the sense of its actual existence dawns upon us. . . .

Taste is the intermediate faculty which connects the active with the passive powers of our nature, the intellect with the senses ; and its appointed function is to elevate the *images* of the latter, while it realises the *ideas* of the former. We must therefore have learned what is peculiar to each before we understand that " Third something " which is formed by a harmony of both. . . .

To express in one word what belongs to the senses or the recipient and more passive faculty of the soul, I have reintroduced the word *sensuous*, used, among many others of our elder writers, by Milton, in his exquisite definition of poetry, as " simple, sensuous, passionate . . ."; thus too I have restored the words *intuition* and *intuitive* to their original sense—" an intuition," says Hooker, " that is a direct and immediate beholding, a presentation of an object to the mind through the senses and imagination."

COLERIDGE

(94)

Every author, as far as he is great, and at the same time *original*, has had the task of *creating* the taste by which he is to be enjoyed ; so has it been, so will it continue to be. . . . The predecessors of an Original Genius of a high order will have smoothed the way for all that he has in common with them—and much he will have in common ; but, for what is peculiarly his own, he will be called upon to clear, and often to shape, his own road : he will be in the condition of Hannibal among the Alps.

And where lies the real difficulty of creating that taste by which a truly original poet is to be relished ? Is it in breaking the bonds of custom, in overcoming the prejudices of false refinement, and displacing the aversions of inexperience ? . . . Does it lie in establishing that dominion over the spirits of readers by which they are to be humbled and humanised in order that they may be purified and exalted ?

If these ends are to be attained by the mere communication of *knowledge*, it does not lie here. TASTE, . . . like IMAGINATION, is a word which has been forced to extend its services far beyond the point to which philosophy would have confined them. It is a metaphor taken from a *passive* sense of the human body, and transferred to things, which are in their essence, *not* passive—to intellectual *acts* and *operations*. . . . But the profound and the exquisite in feeling, the lofty and universal in thought and imagination . . . are neither of them, accurately speaking, objects of a faculty which could ever without a sinking in the spirit of Nations have been designated by the metaphor—*Taste*. And why ? Because without the exertion of a co-operating *power* in the mind of the Reader, there can be no adequate sympathy with either of these emotions : without this auxiliary impulse, elevated or profound, passion cannot exist. . . . To be moved, then, by a passion, is to be excited often to external, and always to internal, effort ; whether for the continuance and strengthening of the passion, or for its suppression, according as the course which it takes may be painful or pleasurable. If the latter, the soul must contribute to its support, or it never becomes vivid—and soon languishes or dies. And this brings us to the point. Every great poet . . . in the highest exercise of his genius, before he can be thoroughly enjoyed, has to call forth and communicate *power*. . . .

Of genius in the fine arts, the only infallible sign is the widening of the sphere of human sensibility, for the delight, honour, and benefit of human nature. Genius is the introduction of a new element into the intellectual universe, or, if that be not allowed, it is the application of powers to objects on which they have not before been exercised, or the employment of them in such a manner as to produce effects hitherto unknown. What is all this but an advance, or a conquest, made by the soul of the poet? Is it to be supposed that the reader can make progress of this kind, like an Indian prince or general, stretched on his palanquin and borne by his slaves? No; he is invigorated and inspired by his leader, in order that he may exert himself; for he cannot proceed in quiescence, he cannot be carried like a dead weight. Therefore to create taste is to call forth and bestow power, of which knowledge is the effect. . . .

Away, then, with the senseless iteration of the word *popular*, applied to new works in poetry, as if there were no test of excellence in this first of the fine arts but that all men should run after its productions, as if urged by an appetite or constrained by a spell. Go to a silent exhibition of the productions of the sister art, and be convinced that the qualities which dazzle at first sight, and kindle the admiration of the multitude, are essentially different from those by which permanent influence is secured.

WORDSWORTH

(95)

All art is the expression of ideas in some sensuous material or medium, and the ideas, in taking material forms of beauty, make a direct appeal to the emotions through the senses.

ROBERT BRIDGES

(96)

Our Schools of Art are confused by the various teachings and various interests that are now abroad amongst us. Everybody is talking about art, and writing about it, and more or less interested in it; everybody wants art, and there is not art for everybody, and few who talk know what they are talking about; thus students are led in all variable ways, while there is only one way in which they can make steady progress, for true art is always and will be always one. Whatever changes may be made in the customs of society, whatever new machines we may invent . . . Fine Art must remain what it was two thousand years ago, in the days of Phidias; two thousand years hence, it will be, in all its principles, and in all its great effects upon the mind of man, just the same.

RUSKIN

(97)

No artist of any art has his complete meaning alone. His significance, his appreciation, is the appreciation of his relation to the dead . . . artists. You cannot value him alone; you must set him, for contrast and comparison, among the dead. I mean this as a principle of æsthetic, not merely historical criticism. The necessity that he shall conform, that he shall cohere, is not one-sided; what happens when a new work of art is created is something that happens simultaneously to all the works of art which preceded it. The existing monuments form an ideal order among themselves, which is modified by the introduction of the new (the really new) work of art among them. The existing order is complete before the new work of art arrives; for order to persist after the supervention of novelty, the *whole* existing order must be, if ever so slightly, altered; and so the relations, proportions, values of each work of art toward the whole are readjusted; and this is conformity between the old and the new. Whoever has approved this idea of order . . . will not find it preposterous that the past should be altered by the present as much as the present is directed by the past. . . .

In a peculiar sense he (the poet or artist) will be aware also that he must inevitably be judged by the standards of the past. I say judged, not amputated, by them; not judged to be as good as, or worse or better than, the dead; and certainly not judged by the canons of dead critics. It is a judgment, a comparison, in which two things are measured by each other. To conform merely would be for the new work not really to conform at all; it would not be new and would therefore not be a work of art. And we do not quite say that the new is more valuable because it fits in; but its fitting in is a test of its value—a test, it is true, which can only be slowly and cautiously applied, for we are none of us infallible judges of conformity. We say: it appears to conform, and is perhaps individual, or it appears individual and may conform; but we are hardly likely to find that it is one and not the other. . . .

The effect of a work of art upon the person who enjoys it is an experience different in kind from any experience not of art.

T. S. Eliot

(98)

Every work of art aims at showing us life and things as they are in truth, but cannot be directly discerned by every one through the mist of objective and subjective contingencies. Art takes away this mist.

The works of the poets, sculptors, and representable artists in general, contain an unacknowledged treasure of profound wisdom; just because out of them the nature of things itself speaks, whose utterances they merely interpret by illustrations and purer repetitions. On this account, however, every one who reads the poem or looks at the picture must certainly contribute out of his own means to bring that wisdom to light; accordingly he comprehends only so much of it as his capacity and culture admit of; as in the deep sea each sailor only lets down the lead as far as the length of the line will allow. Before a picture as before a prince, every one must stand, waiting to see whether and what it will speak to him; and as in the case of a prince, so here he must not himself address it, for then he would only hear himself. . . .

We are only perfectly satisfied by the impression of a work of art when it leaves something which, with all our thinking about it, we cannot bring down to the distinctness of a conception. The mark of that hybrid origin from mere conceptions is that the author of the work of art could, before he set about it, give in distinct words what he intended to present; for then it would have been possible to attain his whole end through these words. Certainly an artist ought to think in the arranging of his work; but only that thought which was *perceived* before it was thought has afterwards, in its communication, the power of animating or rousing, and therefore becomes imperishable.

Schopenhauer

(99)

All great art is the work of the whole living creature, body and soul, and chiefly of the soul. But it is not only *the work* of the whole creature, it likewise *addresses* the whole creature. That in which the perfect being speaks must also have the perfect being to listen. I am not to spend my utmost spirit, and give all my strength and life to my work, while you, spectator or hearer, will give me only the attention of half your soul. You must be all mine, as I am all yours ; it is the only condition on which we can meet each other. All your faculties, all that is in you of greatest and best, must be awake in you, or I have no reward. The painter is not to cast the entire treasure of his human nature into his labour merely to please a part of the beholder ; not merely to delight his senses, not merely to amuse his fancy ; not merely to beguile him into emotion, not merely to lead him into thought ; but to do *all* this. Senses, fancy, feeling, reason, the whole of the beholding spirit, must be stilled in attention or stirred with delight ; else the labouring spirit has not done its work well. For observe, it is not merely its *right* to be thus met, face to face, heart to heart ; but it is its *duty* to evoke this answering of the other soul ; its trumpet call must be so clear, that though the challenge may by dullness or indolence be unanswered, there shall be no error as to the meaning of the appeal ; there must be a summons in the work, which it shall be our own fault if we do not obey. We require this of it, we beseech this of it. Most men do not know what is in them till they receive this summons from their fellows : their hearts die within them, sleep settles upon them, the lethargy of the world's miasmata ; there is nothing for which they are so thankful as the cry, " Awake, thou that sleepest ! " And this cry must be most loudly uttered to their noblest faculties : first of all, to the imagination, for that is the most tender, and the soonest struck into numbness by the poisoned air ; so that one of the main functions of art, in its service to man, is to rouse the imagination from its palsy, like the angel troubling the Bethesda pool ; and the art which does not do this is false to its duty, and degraded in its nature. It is not enough that it be well imagined, it must task the beholder also to imagine well ; and this so imperatively, that if he does not choose to rouse himself to meet the work, he shall not taste it, nor enjoy it in any wise. Once that he is well awake, the guidance which the artist gives him should be full and authoritative : the beholder's imagination should not be suffered to take its own way, or wander hither and thither ; but neither must it be left at rest ; and the right point of realisation, for any given work of art, is that which will enable the spectator to complete it for himself, in the exact way the artist would have him, but not that which will save him the trouble of effecting the completion. So soon as the idea is entirely conveyed, the artist's labour should cease ; and every touch which he adds beyond the point when, with the help of the beholder's imagination, the story ought to have been told, is a degradation to his work. . . .

All true finish consists in the addition of ideas, that is to say, in giving the imagination more food ; for once well awakened, it is ravenous for food.   RUSKIN

(100)

Let us suppose Milton, in company with some stern and prejudiced Puritan, contemplating the front of York Cathedral, and at length expressing his admiration of its beauty. We will suppose it too at that time of his life, when his religious opinions, feelings, and prejudices most nearly coincided with those of the rigid Anti-prelatists.

P. : Beauty ; I am sure it is not the beauty of holiness.

M. : True ; but yet it is beautiful.

P. : It delights me not. What is it good for ? Is it of any use but to be stared at ?

M. : Perhaps not ! But still it is beautiful.

P. : But call to mind the pride and wanton vanity of those cruel shavelings, that wasted the labour and substance of so many thousand poor creatures in the erection of this haughty pile.

M. : I do, but still it is very beautiful.

P. : Think how many score of places of worship, incomparably better suited both for prayer and preaching, and how many faithful ministers might have been maintained, to the blessing of tens of thousands, to them and their children's children, with the treasures lavished on this worthless mass of stone and cement.

M. : Too true ! but nevertheless it is *very* beautiful.

P. : And it is not merely useless, but it feeds the pride of the prelates, and keeps alive the popish and carnal spirit among the people.

M. : Even so, and I presume not to question the wisdom, nor detract from the pious zeal of the first Reformers of Scotland, who for these reasons, destroyed so many fabrics, scarce inferior in beauty to this now before our eyes. But I did not call it *good*, nor have I told thee, brother, that if this were levelled with the ground and existed only in the works of the modeller or engraver, that I should desire to reconstruct it. The GOOD consists in the congruity of a thing with the laws of the reason and the nature of the will, and its fitness to determine the latter to actualise the former ; and it is always discursive. The Beautiful arises from the perceived harmony of an object, whether sight or sound, with the inborn and constitutive rules of the judgment and imagination ; and it is always intuitive. As light to the eye, even such is beauty to the mind, which cannot but have complacency in whatever is perceived as pre-configured to its living faculties. Hence the Greeks called a beautiful object, καλόν quasi καλοῦν, *i.e. calling on* the soul, which receives instantly and welcomes it as something connatural.   COLERIDGE

(101)

We entered the Salon Carré. He planted himself before " The Wedding at Cana." . . . His coat and his melon trailed on the ground. He seemed to be in an ecstasy.

" Here is painting. The part, the whole, the volumes, the values, the composition, the emotional quiver, everything is there. . . . Listen a minute, it's stunning ! . . . Where are we ? Shut your eyes, wait, think of nothing. Now, open them. . . . Isn't it so ? One sees nothing but a great coloured undulation. What then ? An irradiation and glory of colour. That is what a picture should give us, a warm harmony, an abyss in which the eye is lost, a secret germination, a coloured state of grace. All these tones circulate in the blood, don't they? One is revivified, born into the real world, one finds oneself, one becomes the painting. To love a painting, one must have first drunk deeply of it in long draughts. Lose consciousness. Descend with the painter into the dim, tangled roots of things, and rise again from them in the colours, be steeped in the light with them. Know how to see, above all to feel, before a great construction such as Veronese builds. . . . He was happy, that man, and all who understand him become happy.

" . . . What I see is a formidable craft, and one that for them was such an easy and natural one. They had all that in their hands and eyes, handed on from workshop to workshop. . . . He prepared an immense grey design, the naked idea, anatomical, the living skeleton of his universe, the harmonious and inevitable framework to be clothed with tones, with his colours and glazings, in piling up the shadows. To-day we have lost this scientific preparation, this fluid vigour, that is given by the under-painting. Look at this dress, this woman, the creature against this cloth where the shadow begins beneath her smile, where the light caresses her, enfolds her. . . . Each tone penetrates the next, all the volumes moving as they interlace. What continuity! . . . It's magnificent to bathe a boundless and immense composition like this in the same clear and warm light, and to give the eye the vivid impression that all those bosoms are really breathing there, as you and I are breathing here, the golden air that wraps them round. . . . Heavens! the perfect elegance, the exquisite elegance, the daringness of all these flowered stuffs, the stuffs that relate each to the other, the arabesques which interlace, the flowing gestures. Is that enough? You can dwell on the details, but all the rest of the picture will pursue you, and will be with you always. You will feel its clamour permeating your mind from the scrap that you are studying. You can take nothing from the whole. They were not painters of scraps, those men, as we are. . . . Look, let your eyes follow the complete curve of that table. Isn't it beautiful? Isn't it alive? And at the same time isn't it transfigured, miraculous, alive, in another, and yet a real world? The miracle is there, the water is turned to wine, the world changed to painting. One is intoxicated, one is happy. For me it is as if a coloured music carried me along, as if music caressed my face. All my craft runs in my blood. Oh, they had a sacred craft, those old rascals. . . .

" One does not love (these pictures by Veronese) if one looks for literature in them, if one gets excited over the anecdote, the subject. . . . I detest all that, these histories, that psychology, these excrescences. Heavens! all that is in the picture, painters aren't imbeciles, but one must see it with the eyes—with the eyes, don't you understand! The painter desires nothing else. His psychology is the relationship of his tones. That is where his emotion lies. That is his personal history, his truth, his profoundness. Because, don't you see, he's a painter. Neither poet nor philosopher. Michael Angelo did not place his sonnets on the Sistine, any more than Giotto put his *canzone* into the life of St. Francis. . . . Reality is always natural, and has a sensuous significance that is universal, if one dares to say so."

CÉZANNE *to* GASQUET

(102)

I remember seeing an English couple sit for more than an hour on a piercing February day in the Academy at Venice before the celebrated " Assumption " by Titian; and when

I, after being chased from room to room by the cold, concluded to get into the sunshine as fast as possible and let the pictures go, but before leaving, drew reverently near to them to learn with what superior forms of susceptibility they might be endowed, all I overheard was the woman's voice murmuring : " What a *deprecatory* expression her face wears ! What self-*abnegation* ! How *unworthy* she feels of the honour she is receiving ! " Their honest hearts had been kept warm all the while by a glow of spurious sentiment that would have fairly made old Titian sick.

Mr. Ruskin somewhere makes the (for him terrible) admission that religious people, as a rule, care little for pictures, and that when they do care for them they generally prefer the worst ones to the best. WILLIAM JAMES

(103)

Good painting is a music and a melody which intellect only appreciates and with great difficulty. This painting is so rare that few are capable of attaining it. . . .
MICHAEL ANGELO BUONARROTI

(104)

It is the lowest style only of arts, whether of Painting, Poetry, or Musick, that may be said, in the vulgar sense, to be naturally pleasing. The higher efforts of these arts, we know by experience, do not affect minds wholly uncultivated. This refined taste is the consequence of education and habit ; we are born only with a capacity of entertaining this refinement, as we are born with a disposition to receive all rules and regulations of society ; and so far it may be said to be natural to us, and no further. . . . An ignorant uneducated man may, like Apelles's critick, be a competent judge of the truth of the representation of a sandal . . . but a critick in the higher style of art ought to possess the same refined taste, which directed the Artist in his work.
SIR JOSHUA REYNOLDS

(105)

The public can distinguish very readily—far better than it is given credit for—between bad literature and good ; nor is the public deaf to good music, but the public seems quite powerless to distinguish between good painting and bad. No, I am wrong. It distinguishes very readily between bad painting and good, but it invariably prefers the bad. . . . If I could only make folk understand how illusory is their belief, what a service I should render to art ; if I could only make them understand that the original taste of man is always for the commonplace, and that it is only by great labour and care that man learns to understand as beautiful that which the uneducated eye considers ugly.
GEORGE MOORE

(106)

The fact is, that the greater number of persons or societies throughout Europe, whom wealth, or chance, or inheritance has put in possession of valuable pictures, do not know a good picture from a bad one, and have no idea in what the value of a picture really consists. The reputation of certain works is raised, partly by accident, partly by the just testimony of artists, partly by the various and generally bad taste of the public (no picture that I know of, has ever, in modern times, attained popularity, in the full sense of the term, without having some exceedingly bad qualities mingled with its good ones), and when this reputation has once been completely established, it little matters to what state the picture may be reduced : few minds are so completely devoid of imagination as to be unable to invest it with the beauties which they have heard attributed to it.

This being so, the pictures that are most valued are for the most part by those masters of established renown, which are highly or neatly finished, and of a size small enough to admit of their being placed in galleries or saloons, so as to be made subjects of ostentation, and to be easily seen by a crowd. For the support of the fame and value of such pictures, little more is necessary than that they should be kept bright, partly by cleaning, which is incipient destruction, and partly by what is called " restoring," that is, painting over, which is, of course, total destruction. . . .

On the other hand, the most precious works of any noble painter are those which have been done quickly, and in the heat of the first thought, on a large scale, for places where there was little likelihood of their being seen well, or for patrons from whom there was little prospect of rich remuneration. In general, the best things are done in this way, or else in the enthusiasm and pride of accomplishing some great purpose, such as painting a cathedral, or a Campo Santo, from one end to another. . . . They are . . . almost universally neglected, whitewashed by custodes, shot at by soldiers, suffered to drop from the walls piecemeal in powder and rags by society in general.

RUSKIN

(107)

In my time (1823) there was even discovered in Florence a Madonna of Raphael's which had hung for a long series of years on the wall of the servants' hall of a palace (in the *Quartiere de S. Spirito*) ; and this happens among Italians, the nation which is gifted among all others with a sense of the beautiful. It shows how little direct and immediate effect the works of plastic and pictorial art have, and that it requires more culture and knowledge to prize them than the works of all other arts.

SCHOPENHAUER

(108)

Now the right way to go to work—strange as it may appear—is to look at pictures until you have acquired the power of seeing them. If you look at several thousand good pictures every year, and form some sort of practical judgment about every one of them —were it only that it is not worth troubling over—then at the end of five years or so you will, if you have a wise eye, be able to see what is actually in a picture, and not what you think is in it. . . . And so on with all the arts.

GEORGE BERNARD SHAW

(109)

I ask every honest man, provided that he has travelled and thought a little . . . what a modern Winckelmann would say if faced with a Chinese production, a strange, bizarre production, contorted in form, intense in colour, sometimes ethereal almost to vanishing-point ? Yet it is a sample of universal beauty ; but before it can be understood, the critic, the spectator, must bring about a mysterious transformation in himself, until by the phenomenon of will, acting upon imagination, he teaches himself how to live

5

in the heart that has given birth to this isolated phenomenon. Few men have completely
this divine grace of cosmopolitanism ; but all can acquire it in varying degrees.

BAUDELAIRE

(110)

We have to admit . . . that of all that among us is termed the art of the upper
classes—of all those novels, stories, dramas, comedies, pictures, sculptures, symphonies,
operas, operettas, ballets, etc., which profess to be works of art—scarcely one in a hundred
thousand proceeds from an emotion felt by its author, all the rest being but manufactured
counterfeits of art, in which borrowing, imitating, effects, and interestingness, replace the
contagion of feeling. That the proportion of real productions of art is to the counterfeit
is as one to some hundreds of thousands or even more, may be seen by the following
calculation. I have read somewhere that the artist painters of Paris alone number
30,000 ; there will probably be as many in England, as many in Germany, and as many
in Russia, Italy, and the smaller states combined. So that in all there will be in Europe
say 120,000 painters ; and there are probably as many musicians and as many literary
artists. If these 360,000 produce three works a year each (and many of them produce
ten or more), then each year yields over a million so-called works of art. How many,
then, must have been produced in the last ten years ? . . . Evidently millions. Yet
who of all the connoisseurs of art has received impressions from all these pseudo works of
art ? . . . It is usually said that without this enormous number of unsuccessful attempts
we should not have the real works of art. But such reasoning is as though a baker, in
reply to a reproach that his bread was bad, were to say that if it were not for the hundreds
of spoiled loaves there would not be any well-baked ones. . . .

We are surrounded by productions considered artistic. Thousands of verses, thousands of poems, thousands of novels, thousands of dramas, thousands of pictures, thousands of musical pieces, follow after one another. All the verses describe love of nature, or
the author's state of mind, and in all of them rhyme or rhythm is observed. All the
dramas and comedies are splendidly mounted and are performed by admirably trained
actors. All the novels are divided into chapters, all of them describe love, contain effective
situations, and correctly describe the details of life. All the symphonies contain *allegro*,
andante, *scherzo*, and *finale* ; all consist of modulations and chords and are played by
highly trained musicians. All the pictures, in gold frames, saliently depict faces and
sundry accessories. But among these productions in the various branches of art there is
in each branch one among hundreds of thousands, not only somewhat better than the
rest, but differing from them as a diamond differs from paste. The one is priceless, the
others not only have no value but are worse than useless, for they deceive and pervert
taste. And yet, externally, they are to a man of perverted or atrophied artistic perception, precisely alike.

In our society the difficulty of recognising real works of art is further increased by the
fact that the external quality of the work in false productions is not only no worse, but
often better, than in real ones ; the counterfeit is often more effective than the real, and
its subject more interesting. . . .

. . . People sit for whole hours in concert rooms and theatres listening to the new composers, consider it a duty to read the novels of the famous modern novelists, and to look at pictures representing either something incomprehensible or just the very things they see much better in real life ; and above all, they consider it incumbent on them to be enraptured by all this, imagining it all to be art, while at the same time they will pass real works of art by, not only without attention, but even with contempt, merely because in their circle, these works are not included in the list of works of art.   TOLSTOY

(111)

A revolt . . . against the established style, instead of being received with the derision which is generally its fate, should be welcomed as the one possible source from which the arts may derive new vitality.   Not that mere novelty must of necessity be admirable. . . .

I believe it would be no bad rule for the collector who wishes to discover rising talent to confine his study to those works of young men which were consistently damned by the critics of the baser sort as incomplete and ugly. . . .

The rock on which generation after generation of inconsiderate critics, and in particular all academies of the Fine Arts, have come to grief, is the habit of judging new works of art by some fixed standard of grace, or power, or proportion, established and determined by pictures already in existence.   New pictures which correspond in some considerable degree to such a standard are therefore at once acclaimed as masterpieces ; those that differ radically from this accepted standard are called ugly.   In reality this correspondence with some existing standard of grace, or power, or proportion, is not a merit but a fatal defect.   It implies imitation, and no great artist ever was an imitator after his student days.   The great artist invariably departs in some degree from the canons and standards of his own age, and by that departure creates a new quality which is first suspected for eccentricity, or attacked as ugliness ; but which in time is understood, becomes in its turn a standard, and is everywhere recognised as beauty.   C. J. HOLMES

(112)

THE ENCOURAGEMENT OF THE ARTS IN MODERN EUROPE
THE WELCOME GIVEN TO THE PRE-RAPHAELITE MOVEMENT
(Pictures by Ford Madox Brown, Holman Hunt, Rossetti, Millais, etc.)

This school of English youths has, it may be granted, ambition. . . .   Their ambition is an unhealthy thirst which seeks *notoriety* by means of mere conceit.   Abruptness, singularity, uncouthness, are the counters by which they play for fame.   Their trick is to defy the principles of beauty and the recognised axioms of taste. . . . (In certain paintings by Italian primitives) the disgusting incidents of unwashed bodies were not presented in loathsome reality, and flesh, with its incidents of putridity, was not made the affected medium of religious sentiment in tasteless revelation. . . .

Mr. Millais, in his picture . . . which represents a Holy Family in the interior of a carpenter's shop,[1] has been the most successful in the least dignified features of his pre-

[1] See Fig. 38.

sentment, and in giving to the higher forms, characters, and meanings a circumstantial art-language from which we recoil in horror and disgust. There are many to whom his work will seem a pictorial blasphemy. Great talents have here been perverted to the use of an eccentricity both lamentable and revolting.

A ROYAL ACADEMICIAN, in *The Athenæum*, June 1, 1850

You come—in the Royal Academy Exhibition . . . to the contemplation of a Holy Family. You will have the goodness to discharge from your minds all Post-Raphael ideas, all religious aspirations, all elevating thoughts ; all tender, awful, sorrowful, ennobling, sacred, graceful, or beautiful associations ; and prepare yourselves, as befits such a subject—Pre-Raphaelly considered—for the lowest depths of what is mean, odious, repulsive, and revolting.

You behold the interior of a carpenter's shop. In the foreground . . . is a hideous, wry-necked, blubbering, red-headed boy, in a bed-gown, who appears to have received a poke in the hand from the stick of another boy with whom he has been playing in an adjacent gutter, and to be holding it up for the contemplation of a kneeling woman so horrible in her ugliness, that (supposing it were possible for any human creature to exist for a moment with that dislocated throat) she would stand out from the rest of the company as a Monster, in the vilest cabaret in France, or the lowest gin-shop in England. . . . Whenever it is possible to express ugliness of feature, limb, or attitude, you have it expressed. Such men as the carpenters might be undressed in any hospital where dirty drunkards in a high state of varicose veins, are received.

. . . This, in the nineteenth century, and in the eighty-second year of the annual exhibition of the National Academy of Art, is what Pre-Raphaelite Art can do to render reverence and homage to the faith in which we live and die ! . . .

. . . We should be certain of the Plague, among many other advantages, if this Brotherhood were properly encouraged.

CHARLES DICKENS, in *Household Words*, June 15, 1850

THE WELCOME GIVEN TO THE IMPRESSIONIST MOVEMENT

(Pictures by Monet, Cézanne, Renoir, Sisley, Pissarro, Berthe Morisot, etc. For picture by Renoir, see Fig. 157 ; by Cézanne, Figs. 15, 73, 90, 179)

(The pictures) provoke laughter and yet they are lamentable. They display the profoundest ignorance of drawing, of composition, and of colour. When children amuse themselves with a box of colours and a piece of paper they do better.

ROGER BELLUE, in *Le Chronique des Arts et de la Curiosité*, April 1877

The Rue Peletier is unfortunate. Following upon the burning of the opera-house, a new disaster has fallen on the quarter. There has just been opened at M. Durand Ruels' an exhibition which is said to be painting. The innocent passer-by enters and a cruel spectacle meets his terrified gaze. Here five or six lunatics, of whom one is a woman, have chosen to exhibit their works.

There are people who burst into laughter in front of these objects. Personally I am saddened by them. These so-called artists style themselves Intransigeants, Impressionists. They take paint, brush, and canvas. They throw a few colours at the canvas at random and then they sign the lot. In the same way the inmates of a mad-house pick up the stones on the road and think they are diamonds.

ALBERT WOLFF, in *Le Figaro*, April 3, 1876

The Welcome given to the " Post-Impressionist " Movement

(Pictures by Cézanne, Gaugin, Van Gogh, Henri-Matisse, Picasso, etc. For picture by Van Gogh, see Fig. 106 ; by Henri-Matisse, Fig. 31 ; by Picasso, Fig. 72)

A date more favourable than the fifth of November for revealing the existence of a widespread plot to destroy the whole fabric of European painting, could hardly have been chosen. . . . There is no doubt whatever that the vast majority of the pictures . . . will be greeted by the public with a . . . damning and . . . permanent ridicule. When the first shock of merriment has been experienced, there must follow, too, a certain feeling of sadness that distinguished critics, whose profound knowledge and connoisseurship are beyond question, should be found to welcome pretension and imposture. . . .

. . . If the movement is spreading . . . it should be treated like the rat plague in Suffolk. The source of the infection (*e.g.* the pictures) ought to be destroyed.

ROBERT ROSS, in *The Morning Post*, November 7, 1910

(The works) showed intellectual, emotional, and technical degeneracy ; wilful anarchy and notoriety-hunting, which, were it not transparent, might be compared with criminality.

Poor Manet ! It is scarcely fair to attribute the parentage of this rotten egotism to him, a disagreeable artist, a brutal painter, yet a man of genius. . . . Cézanne might well be the father of the Post-Impressionists. Mr. Ross thinks he might have become an artist. I differ. Cézanne mistook his vocation. He should have been a butcher. . . . One will try and forget the joyless and melancholy exhibition. . . . It was a relief to breathe the petroleum-ladened air of Bond Street ; even the chill of a November afternoon became invigorating as a kind of message of health after the suffocating tomb containing scarcely even the ashes of intelligence. For a moment there came even a fierce feeling of terror lest the youth of England, young promising fellows, might be contaminated here. . . .

It would be nauseating to myself and your readers to dwell on details. It would be almost as unpleasant to read as to see. There is no fear for permanent mischief, I hope. The thing is too bad for that. There is no regeneration for deluded egoists. They are morally lost in the inferno where Dante places the unfaithful to God. . . .

I hope the press will teem with resentment against the insults offered to the noble arts of Design, Sculpture, and Painting, an insult, also, to the taste of the English people. . . . This invasion of depressing rubbish is, thank heaven, new to our island of sensible, and in their own fashion, poetic, people.

W. B. RICHMOND, in *The Morning Post*, November 16, 1910

(113)

EDITORIAL FROM *The Burlington Magazine*, July 1904

Of the personal questions involved in the appointment to the curatorship of the Walker Art Gallery, we have no knowledge. The facts are that the art committee of the Liverpool Corporation first selected three out of the sixty-two applicants for the position, and then recommended one of the three to the Corporation for appointment, but the Corporation refused to accept the recommendation, and referred the matter back to the committee. On these facts we make no comment ; but we cannot pass over the strange objection that was made by one member of the committee to a certain candidate (one of the selected three), particularly since the objection seems to have weighed with the committee and to have affected its recommendation. The objection was that the gentleman in question was an art critic. " A critic," said the objector, " is usually a faddist ; he would probably look to one side of art only, and *would perhaps ' come across ' the committee of the council.*"   In plain English, the curator must not know more about art than the committee, lest his opinion should clash with theirs.

The objection is a striking instance of the dislike of learning and intellect which seems to be fast becoming an English characteristic. There is no civilised country, at any rate in Europe, where a man who knows or thinks too much or who has any higher standard than the man-in-the-street, is so generally suspected and overlooked. This is one reason why artistic and literary criticism in this country has for the most part degenerated into shallow and undiscriminating adulation until any attempt to discriminate is resented as an insult by the majority of people and attributed to spite or " faddism."

It will indeed be lamentable if the appointment to the curatorship of so important a public institution as the Walker Art Gallery is nullified by so stupid a prejudice. Who but a man possessing the critical faculty with the requisite knowledge to back it can possibly be trusted in such a difficult and expert business as the purchase of works of art ? If the Liverpool Corporation is wise it will appoint such a man, whoever he may be, will make him responsible, and will give him a free hand. . . . We have sufficient confidence in the common sense of Liverpool councillors to believe that they will recognise that, if a really competent and instructed art critic " comes across " a committee of business men on the question of the purchase of a picture, the chances are that he will be right and the committee wrong, just as the probability would be the other way if the problem related to electric tramways or the water supply. There is only one safe plan in a case like this : to find a man who can be trusted, to trust him completely, and to make him personally and solely responsible for every purchase. If this were done more frequently, some of our municipal galleries might in time cease to be the sorry farces which many of them are at present.

(114)

ENCOURAGEMENT GIVEN IN THE PAST

Wren was the next Genius that arose. . . . During his Time a most melancholy Opportunity offered for Art to exert itself in the most extraordinary Manner : but the

Calamities of the present circumstances were so great and numerous that the Pleas of Elegancy and Beauty could not be heard ; and Necessity and Conveniency took place of Harmony and Magnificence.

What I mean is this : The Fire of London furnished the most perfect Occasion that can ever happen in any City to rebuild it with Pomp and Regularity : this Wren foresaw, and, as we are told, offered a Scheme for that Purpose which would have made it the Wonder of the World. He proposed to have laid out one large Street from Aldgate to Temple-Bar, in the Middle of which was to have been a large Square, capable of containing the new Church of St. Paul's, with a proper distance for the View all round it ; whereby that huge Building would not have been cooped up as it is at Present, in such a Manner as nowhere to be seen to Advantage at all : but would have had a long and ample Vista at each End. . . . He further proposed to rebuild all the Parish Churches in such a Manner as to be seen at the end of every Vista of Houses, and dispersed in such Distances from each other, as to appear neither too thick nor thin in Prospect, but give a proper heightening to the whole Bulk of the City as it filled the Landscape. Lastly, he proposed to build all the Houses uniform and supported on a Piazza. . . . And by the Water-side, from the Bridge to the Temple, he had plan'd a long and broad Wharf or Key, where he design'd to have rang'd all the Halls that belong to the several Companies of the City, with proper warehouses for Merchants, between, to vary the Edifices, and make it at once one of the most beautiful and most useful Ranges of Structure in the World. But the hurry of Rebuilding, and the Disputes about Property, prevented this glorious Scheme from taking place.

Quoted by CHRISTOPHER WREN, son of SIR CHRISTOPHER WREN

(115)

THE PHILISTINE

CÆSAR (*seeing Apollodorus and calling to him*) : Apollodorus, I leave the art of Egypt in your charge. Remember : Rome loves art and will encourage it ungrudgingly.

APOLLODORUS : I understand, Cæsar. Rome will produce no art itself ; but it will buy up and take away whatever the other nations produce.

CÆSAR : What ! Rome produce no art ! Is peace not an art ? Is war not an art ? Is government not an art ? Is civilisation not an art ? All these we give you in exchange for a few ornaments.
GEORGE BERNARD SHAW

(116)

THE JUDGMENT OF TIME

Even in modern times, no living poet ever arrived at the fulness of his fame ; the jury which sits in judgment upon a poet, belonging as he does to all time, must be composed of his peers ; it must be empanelled by Time from the selectest of the wise of many generations.
SHELLEY

COMMENTARY

The final illustrations (Plates XXXV.–L.) may speak for themselves. Which are true works of art, major or minor ? Which are counterfeits ? The question is to be decided not merely by the light of what has been written, but in the only way by which art can be fully experienced, namely, by imaginative insight and contemplation. We must give up our usual habit of attempting to replace the artist's vision by our own, and must try, instead, to share his experience in so far as this is possible. Putting aside our prejudices, we must follow Schopenhauer's advice (p. 60) and must stand before a picture as before a prince, waiting for it to speak.

In reference to the contrasted illustrations it may be remarked :

(i) That failure to achieve success in a system of largely three-dimensional design does not necessarily result in a good two-dimensional structure.

(ii) That certain " Post-Impressionist " or Cubist products can be as offensive, through extreme affectation, as the follies of the " Art Nouveau " movement.

(iii) That in the examples of lettering, the taint of commercial competition and the decay of the sense of form are clearly exposed.

(iv) That in Figs. 177 and 178, the drawing which expresses the sense of solid forms and their relationship is by another child in Cyprus, aged fifteen, also the daughter of a baker ; while the contrasted drawing is by a recent President of the Royal Academy.

(v) That some of the illustrations (not only in this chapter) show that art can tell a story as well as, or better than, works of counterfeit art or pure description.

(vi) That in connection with this Chapter, Appendix I. should be studied.

CHAPTER VII

THE RELATION OF ART TO RELIGION, MORALITY, AND THE SPIRITUAL LIFE

(117)

THERE is a truth about the nature of man and the nature of the universe which philosophy has established with the thought of centuries, and which philosophy alone can state clearly. This truth can be taught to all and should be known by all. It can be taught gradually to children from their earliest years; and they will be convinced by it the more they are taught it and the more they act upon it. It makes education intelligible because it makes life intelligible; and it is welcomed by every unperverted mind because it answers to the desires of that mind, to the desires of what we call the spirit. . . .

The philosophy of the spirit tells us that the spirit desires three things and desires these for their own sake and not for any further aim beyond them. It desires to do what is right for the sake of doing what is right; to know the truth for the sake of knowing the truth; and it has a third desire which is not so easily stated, but which I will now call the desire for beauty. . . .

If (these desires) are pursued for some ulterior end, they change their nature. If, for instance, I aim at goodness, so that I may profit by it, it is no longer goodness that I aim at, but profit. I may do what is right, but I do it for the sake of something else which I value more than doing what is right. I might do what is wrong for the sake of this something else, if it seemed to me that I could better achieve my purpose so. So if I try to discover the truth that I may profit by it, I am really aiming, not at the truth, but at my own profit. And my aim would lead me to believe what is untrue, if I thought that I should profit by that belief. In fact, the only way to discover truth is to seek it for its own sake, and the only way to do what is right is to do it for its own sake. . . .

The common belief of most teachers and moralists in England is that there is only one activity of the spirit, the moral—that we must do good for the sake of doing good and for no other reason—but that the intellectual and æsthetic activities are subsidiary to the moral, and not really spiritual at all. . . .

The great defect of English thought, which is a result of our lack of philosophy, is that we are always apt to think of everything in terms of something else, and to believe that we have explained it when we have thought of it in terms of something else. Thus, when we say that honesty is the best policy, we are thinking of it in terms of something else, commending it, not as honesty, but as expediency. But honesty is not expediency; it is a moral quality, simply itself, and to be desired for itself; and if you think of it as expediency, you cease to know what it is. So if you tell a boy that honesty is the best policy, you tell him what is often untrue. He finds out for himself soon enough that it is not always the best policy; and he may prefer policy to honesty, because he has never been taught what honesty is, nor why he should prefer it to dishonesty. . . .

Unless I value beauty for its own sake I cannot see or hear or in any way experience beauty. The moralist may wish that it should be otherwise; but he cannot alter the nature of the universe or the mind of man to suit his own purposes. It is part of his moral problem to face the facts of life, and if he teaches others that the facts are what they are not, he is behaving immorally for the sake of morals; which means that he is ceasing to understand the nature of morals.

It is a fact that, if I try to discover the truth for some moral end, I shall probably fail to discover it. My further aim will prevent me from seeing things as they are, and I shall see them as I wish to see them for moral purposes. So it is a fact that I cannot experience beauty for some moral end. The further aim actually hinders the experience, and this is still more clear when we come to the production of beauty in works of art. If the artist tries to produce a work of art so that he may make others good, it is not a work of art that he produces. There is in all of us an intellectual and an æsthetic conscience, as well as a moral conscience; and if I want to be intellectually or æsthetically right, I must obey the intellectual or the æsthetic conscience, just as I must obey the moral conscience if I want to be morally right. . . .

The universe is to be valued because there is truth in it and beauty in it; and we live to discover the truth and the beauty no less than to do what is right. Indeed, we cannot attain to that state of mind in which we shall naturally do what is right unless we are aware of the truth and the beauty of the universe. The moral faculty only works rightly when it is enriched and directed by the other two faculties of the spirit, each exercised for its own sake.

Thus a man who does not believe in the absolute value of truth will fail in sincerity because of his disbelief. It is a fact that, if we are to be good, we must exercise our intellectual faculties to the best of our ability. . . .

Every one does instinctively feel that there is some kinship between goodness, truth, and beauty. The philosophy which insists upon that kinship is not mere empty theorising; it is based upon the universal experience of mankind, and attempts to emphasise and explain a fact of that experience. We do feel always that there is something good in truth, something beautiful in goodness, something true in beauty. And the reason is that all three are the aim of spiritual activities, all three are desired for their own sake and not as means to something else. . . .

It is far more difficult to speak of the æsthetic activity of the spirit than of the moral and intellectual, because neither its nature nor its importance is yet clearly understood. . . . If we try to value a work of art, or any æsthetic experience of reality, for moral reasons, we shall miss the æsthetic experience. If we look at a sunset so that it may affect our conduct, we shall fail to experience it æsthetically, and it will not affect our conduct. For certainly our æsthetic activities, like our intellectual, do affect our conduct. Everything which affects our minds must affect our conduct. But they are æsthetic activities because they are exercised for their own sake ; and, unless we exercise them so, our minds are starved of their æsthetic activities, and our conduct suffers accordingly. There are sound moral reasons for exercising the æsthetic activity ; but still it must be exercised for its own sake or it cannot be exercised at all. . . .

We are further hampered in our effort to understand beauty and the æsthetic activity, because, whereas we know that truth is something that happens to our own minds as a result of our intellectual activity, we suppose that beauty is a quality of things which we see, just as we see that things are square or pink. But beauty, just like truth, is something that happens to our minds as a result of the exercise of the æsthetic activity. . . . Our whole civilisation suffers both morally and intellectually from the suppression of the æsthetic activity. We have philistinism on the one hand, which is a stubborn denial of the value of that activity, and æstheticism on the other, which is a morbid exercise of it and a perverse insistence upon its exclusive value. Æstheticism is a reaction against philistinism, a reaction which is bound to occur whenever the æsthetic activity is denied. There are boys in whom the æsthetic activity is too strong to be suppressed, and they commonly revolt against the exclusive insistence upon the moral activity. Often they think that there is something romantic and delightful in immorality, not because they are wicked, but because they see in morality as it is taught them a mere hindrance to the exercise of that other activity which their spirit desires. Morality, when it ousts the other activities of the spirit, does seem to them immoral, as indeed it is. It starves them, and they fly to the conclusion that the only way to richness and freedom is to deny the absolute value of the moral activity altogether. There they fall into the same error as their teachers, who deny the absolute value of the æsthetic activity ; and their counter-denial is itself a fierce and perverse morality, an attempt to redress the balance. The doctrine of art for art's sake in its last absurdity, when it asserts that man should live for art and for nothing else, is a moral doctrine and a declaration that ordinary morality is immoral. It is a kind of æsthetic puritanism, asserting that man is purely an æsthetic creature, as the puritan asserts that he is purely a moral creature. Both are wrong, and wrong because they are both in blind reaction against some other error. It is the function of education to preserve the pupil from all such reactions by teaching him the absolute value of all his spiritual activities, by making him understand that the aim of his life is to exercise them all. . . .

When I love beauty or truth, I escape from self-love no less than when I love goodness. The human animal desires to escape from its animal prison by means of all kinds of love, by freedom of emotion no less than of action or thought. And it attains to the freedom of emotion when it is aware of beauty. It cannot be aware of beauty except in self-forgetfulness, and it cannot produce beauty except in self-forgetfulness. There is in every human being the passionate desire for this self-forgetfulness, and a passionate delight in it when it comes. . . . Education ought to teach us how to be in love always and what to be in love with. The great things of history have been done by the great lovers, by the saints and men of science and artists ; and the problem of civilisation is to give every man a chance of being a saint, a man of science, or an artist. But this problem cannot be attempted, much less solved, unless men desire to be saints, men of science, and artists, and if they are to desire that continuously and consciously, they must be taught what it means to be these things. We think of the man of science or the artist, if not of the saint, as a being with peculiar gifts, not as one who exercises more precisely and incessantly perhaps, activities which we all ought to exercise. . . . Beauty is not an ornament to life or to the things made by man. It is an essential part of both. The æsthetic activity, when it reveals itself in things made by men, reveals itself in design. . . . It shapes objects as the moral activity shapes actions : and we ought to recognise it in objects and value it, as we recognise and value the moral activity in actions.

A. CLUTTON BROCK

(118)

Here comes in religion, for religion is also an affair of the imaginative life, and though it claims to have a direct effect upon conduct, I do not suppose that the religious person if he were wise would justify religion entirely upon its effect on morality, since that, historically speaking, has not been by any means uniformly advantageous. He would probably say that the religious experience was one which corresponded to certain spiritual capacities of human nature, the exercise of which is in itself good and desirable apart from their effect upon actual life. And so, too, I think the artist might if he chose take a mystical attitude, and declare that the fulness and completeness of the imaginative life he leads may correspond to an existence more real and more important than any that we know of in mortal life.

And in saying that his appeal would find a sympathetic echo in most minds, for most people would, I think, say that the pleasures derived from art were of an altogether different character and more fundamental than merely sensual pleasures, that they did exercise some faculties which are felt to belong to whatever part of us there may be which is not entirely ephemeral and material.

It might even be that from this point of view we should rather justify actual life by its relation to the imaginative, justify nature by its relation to art. I mean by this, that since the imaginative life comes in the course of time to represent more or less what mankind feels to be the completest expression of its own nature, the freest use of its innate capacities, the actual life may be explained and justified in its approximation here and there, however partially and inadequately, to that freer and fuller life.

Before leaving this question of the justification of art, let me put it in another way. The imaginative life of a people has very different levels at different times, and these levels do not always correspond with the general level of the morality of actual life. Thus in the thirteenth century we read of barbarity and cruelty which would shock even us ; we may, I think, admit that our moral level, our general humanity, is decidedly higher to-day, but the level of our imaginative life is incomparably lower ; we are satisfied then with a grossness, a sheer barbarity, and squalor which would have shocked the thirteenth century profoundly. Let us admit the moral gain gladly, but do we not also feel a loss : do we not feel that the average business man would be in every way a more admirable, more respectable being if his imaginative life were not so squalid and incoherent ? And if we admit any loss, then there is some function in human nature, other than a purely ethical one, which is worthy of exercise.

As I understand it, art is one of the chief organs of what, for want of a better word, I must call the spiritual life. It both stimulates and controls these indefinable overtones of the material life of man which all of us at moments feel to have a quality of permanence and reality that does not belong to the rest of our experience. Nature demands with no uncertain voice that the physical needs of the body shall be satisfied first; but we feel that our real human life only begins at the point where that is accomplished.

Art . . . is in violent revolt against the instinctive life, it is expressive of the reflective and fully conscious life.

I think that we all agree that we mean by significant form something other than agreeable arrangements of form, harmonious patterns, and the like. We feel that a work which possesses it is the outcome of an endeavour to express an idea rather than to create a pleasing object. Personally, at least, I always feel that it implies the effort on the part of the artist to bend to our emotional understanding by means of his passionate conviction some intractable material which is alien to our spirit. . . .

As to the value of the æsthetic emotion—it is clearly infinitely removed from those ethical values to which Tolstoy would have confined it. It seems to be as remote from active life and its practical utilities as the most useless mathematical theorem. One can only say that those who experience it feel it to have a peculiar quality of " reality " which makes it a matter of infinite importance in their lives. Any attempt I might make to explain this would probably land me in the depths of mysticism. On the edge of that gulf I stop. ROGER FRY

(119)

Now the basest thought possible concerning him (man) is that he has no spiritual nature; and the foolishest misunderstanding of him possible is, that he has, or should have, no animal nature. For he is nobly animal, nobly spiritual—coherently and irrevocably so; neither part of it may, at its peril, expel, despise, or defy the other. All great art confesses, and worships, both. RUSKIN

(120)

And I remember having read that Cupid, when questioned several times by his mother why he did not attack the Muses, replied that he found them so fair, so fine, so chaste, so modest, and so continually occupied, one in contemplation of the planets, another in meditation upon numbers, another in the measurements of geometric bodies, another in rhetorical invention, another in poetic composition, another in the arrangement of music, that, on approaching them, he unbent his bow, closed his quiver, and extinguished his torch, in shame and fear of hurting them. Then he removed the bandage from his eyes that he might more openly look in their faces, and hear their pleasant songs and poetic odes. In all this he took the greatest pleasure in the world, so that often he felt quite enchanted by their beauty and good graces, and went to sleep in harmony. RABELAIS

(121)

. . . These and corresponding conditions of being are experienced principally by those of the most delicate sensibility and the most enlarged imagination, and the state of mind produced by them is at war with every base desire. SHELLEY

(122)

. . . The . . . real and fundamental part of happiness . . . flows from the senses and imaginative life. This element is what the love of beauty can add to life ; for beauty can also be a cause and a factor of happiness. Yet the happiness of loving beauty is either too sensuous to be staple, or else too ultimate, too sacramental, to be accounted happiness by the worldly mind.

Knowledge, affection, religion, and beauty are not less constant influences in a man's life because his consciousness of them is intermittent. Even when absent, they fill the chambers of the mind with a kind of fragrance. They have a continual efficacy as well as a perennial worth. GEORGE SANTAYANA

(123)

A . . . fundamental error lies in affirming the final objects of the Fine Arts to be pleasure. Every man, however, would shrink from describing Æschylus or Phidias, Milton or Michelangelo, as working for a common end with a tumbler or a rope-dancer. No ! he would say, " the pleasure from the Fine Arts is ennobling, which the other is not." Precisely so : and hence it appears that not pleasure but the sense of power and the illimitable, incarnated, as it were, in pleasure, is the true object of the Fine Arts ; and their final purpose, therefore, as truly as that of Science, and much more directly, the exaltation of our human nature. DE QUINCEY

(124)

Think of it and you will find that so far from Art being immoral, little else except art is moral ; that life without industry is brutality, and industry without art is guilt ; and for the words " good " and " wicked," used of men, you may almost substitute the words " Makers " or " Destroyers." [1] RUSKIN

(125)

He has opened a brilliant dream before the imagination. That is enough : neither archæologist, nor moralist, nor historian, nor politician, can say anything. There is nothing bad in the world of art save that which has no style and no shapeliness. RENAN

(126)

An artistic image . . . is neither morally praiseworthy nor blameworthy. Not only is there no penal code that can condemn an image to prison or to death, but no moral judgment, uttered by a rational person, can make of it its object ; we might just as well judge the square moral or the triangle immoral as the Francesca of Dante immoral

[1] We must conclude that Ruskin referred to industry as a whole and not to any particular industry.

or the Cordelia of Shakespeare moral, for these have a purely artistic function, they are like musical notes in the souls of Dante and Shakespeare. . . .

The artist will always be morally blameless and philosophically uncensorable, even though his art should indicate a low morality and philosophy: in so far as he is an artist, he does not act and does not reason, but poetises, paints, sings, and in short, expresses himself: were we to adopt a different criterion we should return to the condemnation of Homeric poetry, in the manner of the Italian critics of the Seicento and the French critics of the time of the fourteenth Louis, who turned up their noses at what they termed " the manners " of these inebriated, vociferating, violent, cruel, and ill-educated heroes. Criticism of the philosophy underlying Dante's poem is certainly possible, but that criticism will enter the subterranean parts of the art of Dante, as though by undermining, and will leave intact the soil on the surface, which is the art.

. . . Since the poet preserved his passion for art when free from every other passionateness, so he preserves in his art the consciousness of duty (duty towards art), and every poet, in the art of creation, is moral, because he accomplishes a sacred function.

The true artist finds himself big with his theme, he knows not how; he feels the moment of birth drawing near, but he cannot will it, or not will it. If he were to wish to act in opposition to his inspiration, to make an arbitrary choice, if, born Anacreon, he were to wish to sing of Atreus and of Alcides, his lyre would warn him of his mistake, echoing only of Venus and of Love, notwithstanding his efforts to the contrary.

The theme or content cannot, therefore, be practically or morally charged with epithets of praise or blame. . . . When . . . critics rebel against the theme or the content as being unworthy of art and blameworthy, in respect to works which they proclaim to be artistically perfect; if these expressions really are perfect, there is nothing to be done but to leave the artists in peace, for they cannot get inspiration, save from what has made an impression on them. The critics should rather think how they can effect changes in nature and society, in order that those impressions may not exist. If ugliness were to vanish from the world, if universal virtue and felicity were established there, perhaps artists would no longer represent perverse or pessimistic sentiments, but sentiments that are calm, innocent, and joyous, like Arcadians of a real Arcady. But so long as ugliness and turpitude exist in nature and impose themselves on the artist, it is not possible to prevent the expression of these things also; and when it has arisen, *factum infectum fieri nequit.* We speak thus from the æsthetic point of view, and from that of pure æsthetic criticism. . . .

The impossibility of choice of content completes the theorem of the *independence of art,* and is also the only legitimate meaning of the expression *art for art's sake.* Art is thus independent of science, as it is of the useful and the moral. Let it not be feared that thus may be justified art that is frivolous or cold, since that which is truly frivolous or cold is so because it has not been raised to expression; or in other words, frivolity and frigidity come always from the form of the æsthetic elaboration, from the lack of a content, not from the material qualities of the content. CROCE

(127)

The Great Artist

. . . Nothing exists in the world about him, that is not beautiful in his eyes, in one degree or another ; so far as not beautiful it is serviceable to set off beauty ; nothing can possibly present itself to him that is not either lovely, or tractable, and shapeable into loveliness ; there is no Evil in his eyes ; only Good and that which displays good. Light is lovely to him ; but not a whit more precious than shadow—white is pleasant to him, as it is to you and me ; but he differs from you and me in having no less delight in black, when black is where black should be. Graceful and soft forms are indeed a luxury to him ; but he would not thank you for them unless you allowed him also rugged ones. Feasting is consolatory to his system, as to yours and mine, but he differs from us in feeling also an exquisite complacency in Fasting, and taking infinite satisfaction in Emptiness. You can excite his intense gratitude by the gift of Anything, and if you have Nothing to give him, you will find that Nothing is exactly the thing he most wants, and that he will immediately proceed to make half a picture out of it. How can you make such a man as this discontented with the world ? There are Three colours in it—he wants no fourth—finds three quite as much as he can manage. There's good firm ground to set easels on in it—he is not so sure that they would stand so firm upon clouds, or that he could paint flying. But the world is a passing, dreamy, visionary state of things ! Do you then want them to be always the same—how could one vary one's picture if that were so ? But people lose their beauty and get old in the world ! Then they have long beards, nothing can be more picturesque. But people die out of the world ! How else would there be room for the Children in it, and how could one paint without children ? But how unhappy people are in the world ! It must be their own fault surely, I'm not. But how thin and ugly their grief makes them—don't you mourn for the departure of the bloom of youth ? Not at all—I like painting thin people as well as fat ones—one can see their skulls better. But how wicked people are in the world ! is it not dreadful to see such wickedness ? Not at all—it varies the expression of their faces ; there would be no pleasure in painting if they all looked alike. Besides, if there were no wicked people there would be no fighting—no heroes—no armour—no triumphs—one might as well not be a painter at all. But don't you want to mend the world then ? No—I don't see that it wants mending—unless, perhaps, it might be better with fewer fogs in it ; but I don't know, and I daresay fogs are all our own fault for not draining better ; at all events —the best you can do for me at present is to stand out of the light, and let me go on painting.[1]

What can be done with such a man ? How are you to make him care about future things ? Even if misfortune fall upon him, such as would make other people religious, he will not seek for Consolation in Heaven. He will seek it in his painting-room. So long as he can paint, nothing will crush him. Nothing short of blindness—nothing, that is, but his ceasing to be a painter, will enable him to contemplate futurity.

[1] Contrast the more sombre colouring of other pictures of the artist's life.

Nay ;—it may be replied—may he not be led, without suffering, but in his own work and in his own way, to that happy religion which you have admitted to be possible, in which this world may be enjoyed without forgetting the next ? No ; by no manner of means—at least of means hitherto brought to bear in this world's history. As far as we have seen, hitherto, all happy religious life has consisted in the fulfilment of direct social duty—in pure and calm domestic relations—in active charity, or in simply useful occupations, trades, husbandry, such as leave the mind free to dwell on matters connected with the spiritual life. You may have religious shepherds, labourers, farmers, merchants, shopmen, manufacturers—and religious painters, so far as they make themselves manufacturers—so far as they remain painters—no.

For consider the first business of a painter ; half, as I said, of his business in this world must consist in simply seeking his own pleasure, and that, in the main, a sensual pleasure. I don't mean a degrading one, but a bodily, not a spiritual pleasure. Seeing a fine red, or a beautiful line, is a bodily and selfish pleasure, at least as compared with Gratitude or Love—or the other feelings called into play by social action. And moreover, their bodily pleasure must be sought for Itself and Himself. Not for anybody else's sake. Unless a painter works wholly to please himself, he will please nobody ;—he must not be thinking while he is at work of any human creature's likings, but his own. He must not benevolently desire to please any more than ambitiously—neither in kindness, nor in pride, may he defer to other people's sensations. " I alone here, on my inch of earth, paint this thing for my own sole joy, and according to my own sole mind. So I should paint it, if no other human being existed but myself. Let who will get good or ill from this—I am not concerned therewith. Thus I must do it, for thus I see it, and thus I like it, woe be to me if I paint as other people see or like." This is the first law of the painter's being ; ruthless and selfish—cutting him entirely away from all love of his fellow-creatures, till the work is done. When done, he may open the door to them, saying calmly : " If you like this—well, I am glad. If you like it not, away with you, I've nothing for you." No great exertion of benevolence, even in this. But further. To order the pursuit of this beauty rightly, our great painter must not shrink in a timid way from any form of vice or ugliness. He must know them to the full, or he cannot understand the relations of beauty and virtue to them. . . .

And this being so, as the great painter is not allowed to be indignant or exclusive, it is not possible for him to nourish his (so-called) spiritual desires, as it is to an ordinary virtuous person. Your ordinarily good man absolutely avoids, either for fear of getting harm, or because he has no pleasure in such places or people, all scenes that foster vice, and all companies that delight in it. He spends his summer evenings on his own quiet lawn, listening to the blackbirds or singing hymns with his children. But you can't learn to paint of blackbirds, nor by singing hymns. You must be in the wildness of the midnight masque—in the misery of the dark street at dawn—in the crowd when it rages fiercest against law—in the council-chamber when it devises worst against the people— on the moor with the wanderer, or the robber in the boudoir with the delicate recklessness of female guilt—and all this, without being angry at any of these things—without ever losing your temper so much as to make your hand shake, or getting so much of the

6

mist of sorrow in your eyes, as will at all interfere with your matching of colours ; never even allowing yourself to disapprove of anything that anybody enjoys, so far as not to enter into their enjoyment. Does a man get drunk, you must be ready to pledge him. Is he preparing to cut purses—you must go to Gadshill with him—nothing doubting—no wise thinking yourself bound to play the Justice, yet always cool yourself as you either look on, or take any necessary part in the play. Cool, and strong-willed—moveless in observant soul. Does a man die at your feet—your business is not to help him, but to note the colour of his lips ; does a woman embrace her destruction before you, your business is not to save her, but to watch how she bends her arms. Not a specially religious or spiritual business this, it might appear.

And then, lastly. Not only is your painter thus concerned wholly and indiscriminately with the affairs of this world, but the mechanism of his own business is one which must occupy nearly all the thought of his leisure or seclusion. Whatever time others give to meditation, or other beneficial mental exercise, he must give to mere practice of touch, and study of hue. Painting cannot be learned in any other way. So many hours a day of steady practice—all your mind and nervous energy put into it—or no good painting. No genius will exempt you from this law of toil ; a painter's genius especially signifies the love of beauty which will never let him rest in the effort to realise it. A man of science may, if he choose, rest content at any moment with the knowledge he has attained, for however much more he learns, he will be as far from knowing All, as ever he was ; but to a painter, absolute perfectness of skill is an approachable, though not an attainable, goal : every hour that he gives to his work, brings him nearer a conceivable faculty of laying on the exact colour he wants in the exact shape he wants ; he feels himself every day able to do more and more as he would ; and though he knows he can never be absolutely perfect, any more than a continually enlarging circle can become an infinite straight line, still, the straight line is before his eyes, and forces him for ever to strive to reach it more and more nearly. This continual mechanical toil, this fixed physical aim, occupies his intellect and energy at every spare moment—blunts his sorrows, restrains his enthusiasms, limits his speculations, takes away all common chances of his being affected by the feelings or imaginations which lead other men to religion.

RUSKIN

(128)

Up to the age of thirty, or beyond it, poetry of many kinds . . . gave me great pleasure, and even as a schoolboy I took intense delight in Shakespeare, especially in the historical plays. I have also said that formerly pictures gave me considerable, and music very great delight. But now for many years I cannot endure to read a line of poetry ; I have tried lately to read Shakespeare and found it so intolerably dull that it nauseated me. I have also almost lost my taste for pictures and music. . . .

My mind seems to have become a machine for grinding general laws out of large collections of facts : but why it should have caused the atrophy of that part of my brain alone on which the higher tastes depend I cannot conceive. . . . If I had to live my life again I would have made it a rule to read some poetry and to listen to some music at least once a week ; for perhaps the parts of my brain now atrophied would thus have been kept alive through use. The loss of these tastes is a loss of happiness and may probably be injurious to the intellect and more probably to the moral character by enfeebling the emotional part of our nature.   CHARLES DARWIN

(129)

. . . What is immortality but the things relating to the spirit which lives eternally ? . . . Answer this for yourselves and expel from among you those who pretend to despise the labours of Art and Science. . . . He who despises and mocks a mental gift in another, calling it pride and selfishness, mocks Jesus, the giver of every Mental Gift, which always appear to the ignorance-loving Hypocrite as Sins ; but that which is a Sin in the sight of cruel Man is not so in the sight of our kind God. Let every Christian, as much as in him is, engage himself openly and publicly before all the World in some Mental pursuit for the building up of Jerusalem.

When imagination, art, and science, and all intellectual gifts, all gifts of the Holy Ghost, are looked upon as of no use, . . . then the Last Judgment begins.

WILLIAM BLAKE

(130)

. . . Others tried to catch beauty as a butterfly, and pin it down for inspection. . . . But a corpse is not an *entire* animal ; it wants that which is essential in all things, namely, life, spirit, which sheds beauty on everything.   GOETHE

In conclusion, a choice is offered :

(131)

Art is not a superior kind of chemistry amenable to the rules of scientific induction. Its component parts cannot be classified and tested, and there is a spark within it which defies foreknowledge.   LYTTON STRACHEY

(132)

" To hear people speak," said Goethe, " one would almost believe that they were of opinion that God had withdrawn into silence since these old times, and that man was now placed quite upon his own feet, and had to see how he could get on without God, and his daily invisible breath. In religious and moral matters, a divine influence is indeed still allowed, but in matters of science and art it is believed that they are merely earthy, and nothing but the product of human powers.

" Let anyone only try, with human will and human power, to produce something which may be compared with the creations that bear the names of *Mozart, Raphael,* or *Shakespeare.* I know very well that these three noble beings are not the only ones, and that in every province of art innumerable excellent geniuses have operated, who have produced things as perfectly good as those just mentioned. But if they were as great as those, they rose above ordinary human nature and were in the same proportion as divinely endowed as they.

" And after all, what does it come to ?   God did not retire to rest after the well-known six days of creation, but, on the contrary, is constantly active as on the first.   It would have been for Him a poor occupation to compose this heavy world out of simple elements and to keep it rolling in the sunbeams from year to year, if He had not had the plan for founding a nursery for a world of spirits upon this material basis.   So now He is constantly active in higher natures to attract the lower ones."

Goethe was silent.   But I cherished his great and good words in my heart.

Conversations of GOETHE *with* ECKERMANN

APPENDIX I

CHILDREN AND ART: AN EXPERIMENT

BY MARGARET H. BULLEY

(Reprinted from *The Burlington Magazine*, October 1923. The references to Plates and pages have been changed to those of the corresponding Plates and pages in this book.)

IN a previous number of this magazine I described a test made on the reaction of elementary school children to a work of art.[1] I propose to describe here a second and more elaborate test in which 1928 children and 399 adults were confronted with the four pairs of reproductions on Plates LI and LII, and were asked to write down, or in a few cases to state by word of mouth, which of the two pictures in each pair they preferred. Each pair of illustrations has a superficial resemblance of subject and grouping, but are obviously very different in æsthetic value. Our object was to find out whether a child's appreciation of art was influenced by sex, age, or good art teaching, and whether the " cleverer " children in the higher divisions of each form possessed better taste than the children in the lower divisions. Except in certain instances it was impossible to correlate powers of understanding the art of others with creative power. It was obvious that a good picture might be preferred or a bad one rejected for other than æsthetic reasons, including purely negative ones. A child might dislike both the good and the bad pictures on a card—like the small boy of eight who wrote " C is orful and D is hrbal too "—and yet feel obliged to state a preference. For these reasons the test would have little value if applied to a small number of children. But if many hundreds of children in different schools and clubs of a similar type were tested, then anything like constancy of result might be expected to have evidential value.[2]

The chart given on p. 88 shows, in the form of a graph, the result of the test. With the exception of the Dudley High School girls, the children had had only an elementary education. The girls from Dudley came from homes where they had little or no opportunity of seeing art of any sort. Dudley is a typical Black Country town, and the girls' parents for the most part belong to the shop-keeper class. But they have had the great advantage of having been taught by Miss Marion Richardson, who has been art mistress in the school for the last ten years.

Two psychologists, to whom I showed the chart, agreed that the decline in taste that is so marked as the small child grows older is probably due to the fact that the child is then outgrowing its life of fantasy and imagination, and is entering into a phase of extreme realism when it is powerfully attracted by everything practical. At about fourteen the child finds that contact with real life can hurt, and with adolescence it turns once more to fantasy, though in a less marked degree than in early childhood.[3] Appreciation and creation are not of necessity found together. For example, two of the best artists among Miss Richardson's girls made the maximum of four wrong choices in the test. Further, it was proved that in the elementary schools the children in divisions " B " invariably did as well as those in divisions " A "; but at Dudley, where the girls under Miss Richardson had been offered a definite theory of art and an idea to grasp, without exception the " A " girls did better than the " B " ones. The children were allowed to offer reasons for their preferences, and most of them

---

[1] *Burlington Magazine*, No. 199, vol. xxxv., Oct. 1919.

[2] [It may be permissible to anticipate a question not dealt with by Miss Bulley: Had the children any opportunity of discovering which pictures Miss Bulley herself preferred? We are entirely satisfied that that was not so.
—EDITOR.]

[3] This does not necessarily apply to creative power. Miss Richardson and Mr. Keith Baynes testify that some of the best work by their pupils is done during the ages of ten to fourteen. No doubt much depends on the teaching at this time. On the other hand, it may interest some readers to know that according to the findings of M. Coué and the new Nancy School, it is between the ages of about ten and fourteen that boys and girls show least " suggestibility."

chose to do so. The six- and seven-year-olds insisted on it. Often the answers are unilluminating The following, by a boy of six who made the four right choices, is typical : [1]

B he preferred " because of the baby and mother." | E, " because of the trees."
D, " best pattern." | G, " the sky is nice."

Often a child who obviously shows æsthetic sensibility is deterred by an understanding of the sadness, gloom, or strangeness expressed in some of the pictures, which he consequently dislikes. In the following answers a boy of nine has clearly been repelled by the sadness expressed in " B," the gloom and slightly mysterious character of " E," and the fierceness and uncanniness of " G " :

A, " faces prettier and radiant." | F, " pretty, while E is lonely and dreary."
D, " looks like a church window, and C | H, " lighter."
only looks like a wallpaper."

A boy of seven preferred :

B, " bigger than the other." | E, " it is easier."
D, " there is a lot more in it." | H, " it is prettier."

A number of children welcome the familiar. The following are unwitting but biting comments on the sort of " art " that we are used to to-day :

A, " seems more homely " (B10) ; " more fascinable for these days than B " (G11) ; " looks like a real photo " (G14).
F, " more picturesque " (B10) ; " more up-to-date " (B11).

[(B) *or* (G) *followed by a figure mean Boy or Girl, with age.*]

Here we have the type of reason that makes " F " so universally popular, particularly with adults :

F, " it reminds me of the place I lived in for my holidays, with my mother and granny " (B14).

And the small child's equivalent :

E, " because I like playing cowboys " (G7).

By ten, the concepts of art and antiquity begin to affect judgment, and the collector and antiquary appear in embryo.

E, " it is older than F " (B10).
D, " it suggests to me a primeval drawing which I consider interesting " (B14) ; " I would value it because it looks like a piece of tapestry made in olden days " (B12).

Imagined colour is often remarked upon, particularly in connection with D.

D, " it has a good amount of colour in it " (B14) ; " it has pretty colours in it " (G8) ;

and so forth.

Taking the cards in turn, here are a few of the preferences with the remarks made :

A preferred, because " B is only a statue " (G13) ; " it is ecey to do " (B7) ; " both figures sweetly pretty and have exquisite expressions " (G16).
B preferred, because " has more shape and finer expression " (G17) ; " A mother's sympathy is not always told by looks " (B13) ; " the mother is clean " (B8) ; " the baby has nice fat on it " (B7) ; " A is a lot too perfect " (G14).
C and D. The words " pattern " and " design " were continually used in connection with this pair of illustrations, though not of B, E, and G. The youngest children were attracted by the fantastic element in both C and D, particularly in D.
D preferred, because " it is like a circaus under the water " (G9) ; " because of the fishes and fancey work " (B8) ; " it is like the ach of a church " (G6) ; " it has got two reindeer at the end of a pole " (G10) ; " it is like a palace " (G10) ; " it is a sign of friendship. Most other animals would have quarrelled " (B13) ; " there is more in it. The other is just an ordinary picture " (B14) ; " does not look like a real thing pulled out of shape. It is really something new based on a peacock " (G14).
E preferred, because " it is a much neater drawing : F is rough " (B13) ; " it is not rough " (B6) ; " it looks smoother " (B8) ; " not so flat as the other one " (B9) ; " it has nice smooth ground " (B6) ; " it looks cleaner " (B9) ; " you can see it more plainly " (B10) ; " I like F, it has a sunny smile " (B11).

---

[1] The capital letters refer to those printed under the illustrations.

"G" and "H":

G preferred, because "it is not rough" (G6); "more in proportion" (B13); "it is cleaner" (B22); "I like darker shadows better than light shadows" (B8); "it has a darker shadow" (B7); "it is more sensible" (G10); "it is blacker" (B7); "it looks so wild and mysterious" (G11); "the flowers are arranged nicely" (G10); "more in proportion and more life-like" (G10); "not rough and H is blacker" (B7); "it looks so wilde and mysterious" (B8); "because of the colourings, light and dark, you can see the difference" (G14).

H preferred, because "it is not so dreary and miseopol" (B8); "the dog does not look wilde" (G7); "I do not like Egyptian art" (B10); "it has more of a racing dog and I like them because I am a bit of a racer myself" (B14).

The older girls and boys sometimes volunteered remarks. One girl of seventeen chose the right pictures, and when jeered at by another girl said, "Can't you see there is something very important about them?" Another remarked, "The uglier ones have more in them than the pretty ones." Here are some of the preferences and reasons offered by the Dudley High School girls:

"B, more expression, not so pretty looking as A. Simpler and stronger lines. Forms harmony" (18). "E, although not so accurate to nature it has more meaning in it" (18). "D is real and C is only paper. G is just pretty and artificial" (17); "G is real and H is not. H looks more like a diagram than a picture" (17); "D, it has something behind it. B has much more feeling, one can see right through it, while A seems just placed there with no depth whatsoever. There are lovely curves in the face of B. D is much better than C. Strength in it while C seems like a film or like glass, allowing every one to look right through it and see nothing" (17). "C seems to be something that could go on for yard after yard, and D is a complete thing" (16). "F looks like a photograph painted to look pretty. E painted with feeling" (16). "G has more quality in it. The water in H does not give me the mysterious feeling that a pool generally does when looking into it, whereas G does. D makes a more complete pattern. On looking at C one sees the birds individually, not as a whole picture, and I would criticize them as such, whereas D makes a complete harmony" (16). "E, F is a commoner view. E seems as though it had come from the artist's head and imagination. There is more deepness in E" (16). "B, simpler in every way. Forms a harmony of shape. Has more strength" (16). "Deeper richer tone in E than weak-looking F. In G everything seems to go together so well. In H I think the things are put in because they had to be put into the picture somehow" (15). "G: H has been drawn off G and spoilt" (15). (The only one out of 2351 persons tested who remarked upon this.) "B, the faces are beautifully sculptured and the shadow seems to make it more beautiful. The dark and light shadow form a harmony" (15). "G, the one who did it got a clear idea, but in H there seems to be bits of dabs in with no meaning" (15). "B, more of a work of art than A. A chocolate boxy while B seems as if the person who did it had not ever seen any second-hand pictures" (15). "E, it makes you think of something more than a view, as the other appears to be" (15). "G blends together and makes one big tune" (12). "E looks the prettiest and needs no fussy bits to make it look nice" (12).

It is interesting to know that Miss Richardson, of the Dudley High School, attributes the drop in appreciation shown by the girls of seventeen to the fact that they had stopped all "arts" subjects for a year and had concentrated on science.

There are many interesting questions opened up in connection with the results shown by the test, but lack of space makes comment impossible. It is hoped in a future article to publish results obtained in Africa and the East, and in this connection I would be grateful if any reader of this article could put me into touch with anyone interested in æsthetics who would be willing to carry out the test on natives.

In conclusion, the following analysis of choices, arranged in order of votes, may prove of painful interest. Not being taken on a system of proportional representation the record of the first four choices only, in each instance, has value:

Boys' choices: A H C F E D G B.
Girls' choices: A C F H E D G B.
Dudley High School: D A H F E B G C.
Oxford Extension Students (Summer Meeting): F G A D C B H E.
Members of British Psychological Society: F GD (equal votes) B A CH (equal votes) E.
Women from gaol: F ACH (equal votes) BDG (equal votes) E.

NOTE.—For description of illustrations see List of Illustrations, p. 101. It may be added that these test illustrations were shown to six well-known London critics or Directors in public galleries or museums, and that they were all in complete agreement as to the relative artistic value of the contrasted pairs of reproductions. The " thirty men and women with knowledge of art " were people I happened to meet during a few weeks when I was carrying out the test. I knew that they were familiar with genuine works of art of different ages and countries, but only a few of them were artists or art critics. I classified all their choices and deleted no set of answers because it was unsatisfactory. For " Psychological Association " in graph read " Psychological Society."

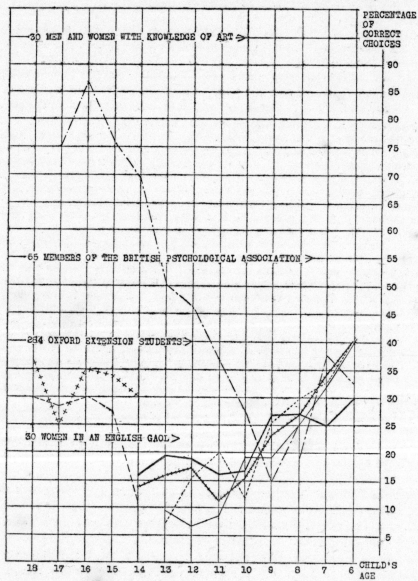

GRAPH SHOWING THE PERCENTAGE OF CORRECT CHOICES MADE BY CHILDREN OF VARIOUS AGES FROM THE FOLLOWING SCHOOLS:

	KEY
340 girls from Dudley High School	———————
184 boys from London Continuation schools and clubs	
186 girls ,, ,, ,, ,, ,, ,, . . .	+++++++++++
202 girls from North Country 1st Elementary School	— — — — — —
278 boys ,, ,, ,, ,, ,, ,, . . .	
391 boys ,, ,, ,, 2nd ,, ,, . . .	++++++++++++++
347 girls ,, ,, ,, ,, ,, ,, . . .	- - - - - - - - - - -

SUPPLEMENT

IT may perhaps be considered of interest if a second edition of the test be added at this point. It can only be a very incomplete addition, for although results of the test have been sent in from various parts of the world, only those from France and Cyprus are yet full enough to be classified and reported upon. But I think it is well that they should be presented for consideration, because they bear out the general tendency of the age-curve as shown in the first graph; and although all the results up to date must only be looked upon as suggestive, and await supplementary experiment and evidence, it does appear probable that a more or less constant result can be expected when dealing with boys and girls from six to eighteen years, in Europe at least.

The graph and key at the end of the Report are largely self-explanatory. The " 2038 girls and boys from English elementary schools " represent the combined children from the elementary schools, continuation schools, and clubs whose averages were given in the graph published by *The Burlington Magazine*, with the addition of 450 boys and girls from a London elementary school. Mr. Diamante Christodoulides very kindly tested the children in Cyprus, while the French children were tested as a result of arrangements kindly made by Mr. Roger Fry and Monsieur Charles Mauron.

English critics will note with sorrow, but without surprise, the low averages of the English children. What the graph does not show is that the London children did rather better in the test than the children in the north. In the same way the taste of the children from Normandy fell below that of the children from Provence, while the children from the small village school of Kiti showed better taste than the children of Nicosia.[1] It is interesting to learn that there is a fine sixth-century (?) mosaic in the church at Kiti. The comparatively small number of results from Japan have been added as suggesting what may happen to Eastern taste when under Western influence.

No reasons for preferences from the children in Cyprus have been given, because only a certain number of these reasons were translated or reported, and those that reached me were not of special interest. It was noticeable, however, that a number of the children disliked the baby in B, because it was blind. On inquiry it turned out that many children in the island suffer from eye disease. As usual with this comparison (A–B), the psychological interest of the subject-matter diverted conscious interest in the question of design, although the southern children were much more fully aware of the sense of reality communicated, and the form of the experience did not prove so great a barrier. The chief difference apparent between northern and southern European preferences was that E was much more popular in the south. The fact that it represented a type of landscape familiar in the south while F is more typical of the north, had probably a good deal to do with this preference, and on this account northern children were slightly handicapped in the test.

COMMENTS BY FRENCH CHILDREN

B preferred, because " I find in it an expression of peace and sincerity, an equilibrium in the composition and in the coloured tones, a greater harmony " (no age given); " in Figure A there is such a common note that one finds in so many pictures " (G15); " one feels a mother's love; they look poor, but love unites them " (B13); " in A the poses are so conventional " (G16); " in A she is unrealisably beautiful " (G15); " one sees that she is a real woman, a human being, and not artificial as A is. Her two hands seem to try and protect the little child from an enemy " (G13); " the mother and child do not look quite so gracious " (G11); " because of the composition, the light, and the more truthful expression of the people " (G18); " though less pretty perhaps, it is truer and more natural. It expresses better the love of all mothers " (G16); " even if more childish in realisation, it is a truer

---

[1] Ages of Kiti children 6–13 years. Only six of these boys were over 10 years old.

rendering. In spite of the gaucheries in the form of the expression it is more natural. A looks more like an illustration. It is the product of imagination rather than observation. In B, on the contrary, the mother and child have the expression of their age " (G18) ; " the mother takes care of her son instead of taking care of herself " (G11) ; " because of the brilliant translation of a mother's love " (G14) ; " she represents a poor mother holding a fretful child, whereas the other represents opulence, because she is a foster-nurse and not the mother " (B13) ; " because my first name begins with a B " (B10) ; " it wrings my heart to think of the certain and deplorable end of these two people " (B17).

A preferred " because it reminds me of my youth and my mother when she was younger " (B10) ; " the mother and the child represent health, gaiety, cleanliness, and beauty " (G12).

D preferred, because " it is infinitely more simple in line, and shows decorative unity and co-ordination and solid richness of line " (G15) ; " the drawing is more sensitive and delicate, and there is greater equilibrium in the masses " (G15) ; " this drawing seems more sympathetic and less proud than the other " (G15) ; " more artistic, better composition, more research, and more personality than C " (G13) ; " it is prettier and more coquettish than C, and there is a pretty border round it, and a black and white horse's collar with big black and white balls, and I like it because it is a crown and C is the republic " (B10) ; " it has needed more architecture to make this picture than the other, and it is less proud than C " (B11) ; " there is a frog in the middle, little dogs, a tortoise in one small corner, and pigeons above " (no age given) ; " the gentleman puts his feet in the air ; because the gentleman is in a circle of lace, and there are two little dogs " (no age given) ; " one sees two turkeys with cherries on their heads. Their wings shimmer with colours, a garland of cherries round, between the two a stick, against which two goats lean, above a fish sparkling like the turkey's, separated by a square piece of wood a little pointed on top " (G11).

E preferred, because " the picture represents a more complete subject " (G14) ; " the trees are more harmonious, and because the view is darker the beauty of the forms comes out better " (G16) ; " this picture is not for ever the same thing as picture F, which one would end by getting tired of " (G12) ; " it gives a greater sense of reality, of movement, of life, and of volume " (G17) ; " the decoration is more original, richer, and the style more majestic than F " (G17) ; " the landscape is truer and less banal, and the trees are better interpreted " (G18) ; " because of the happy repetition of the mountain and plain which gives variety to the landscape and produces a harmonious effect. The landscape is very decorative and there is life in it " (G15) ; " the landscape is beautiful, and seems to me mysterious, and gives an impression of calmness and sweetness " (G15) ; " it forms a picturesque decoration " (G14) ; " it is pretty and curious ; the trees are curiously arranged " (B13) ; " it is artistic and full of harmony. The low hills, the little lake, the ruined castle, and the shadow produced by the great pines give me an impression of severity " (G13).

G preferred, because " the outlines of the drawing are graceful. In the other one they are rigid and heavy " (G13) ; " in H there are faults of proportion " (G15) ; " the composition is better balanced " (G18) ; " the equilibrium of the masses is better and it is more harmonious, and the forms are more ample " (G18) ; " because the thin dog harmonises better with the setting of the scene " (G16) ; " the dog is a better shape " (G15) ; " the decoration is simple and beautiful " (G13) ; " the rocks are more divided up and the plant falls beautifully " (G12) ; " because of the beautiful mountains " (B12) ; " because the ground is more drawn out and better arranged " (B12) ; " the animal is recognisable. In H it is part dog, part horse, part donkey, part camel, and also part ox " (B16).

COMMENTS BY ADDITIONAL LONDON SCHOOL CHILDREN

B preferred, because " it shows you how she loves him so much that it seems as if she is blessing him " (B13) ; " it is darker " (G9).

A preferred because " it makes the picture brighten up because there is no thinking in it " (B11) ; " in this picture they appear more beautiful, which suits their spotless character " (B13) ; " it is of my own nation " (B10).

D preferred, because " the designer has got all the different colours matched together " (G13) ; " although it does not look the actual bird, it is more natural than C " (G13) ; " it is prettier trimed " (G10) ; " it is made to fill the space nicely " (G9) ; " these two birds do not look so proud as the other two, and they are quite content although they are very plain birds " (G12) ; " it looks lifelike, and reminds you of your Christmas dinner " (G13).

C preferred " because anybody can see it and understand it " (B13).

E preferred, because " it is a very lovely picture, but I really haven't got the reason why I like it best " (G12).

G preferred, because " they have got it carved out better " (G12) ; " its tail is not stuck on. Some people do not curve their tails in when they do them, but stick them on " (G12) ; " it is a pretty pattern " (G9) ; " it looks as if the one who made the pattern did it of their own idea and did not draw it from somebody's else's pattern or make it look so real " (G11) ; " because this picture is worth a frame " (G12).

In addition, 694 Jewish children were tested in London schools, and interesting results were obtained. The taste of these children is, on the whole, slightly better than that of other London elementary school children, but not quite as good as that of the French. Although this test is not yet complete enough to be reported upon, a few remarks by the children may be quoted :

B preferred " because it is more fairy-like " (G9).

A preferred " because I like the white woman with her baby better than the black woman with her baby, because the white woman and her baby have English blood and therefore an English boy or girl should chose the white rather than the black " (B12).

D preferred, because " it has a much neater design than C, which looks all over the place ; D has more art in it " (G12) ; " its work looks something out of the ordinary, and is thought out, whereas C is a bird you know " (G12) ; " because its art was more cunningly put than C " (G13) ; " it is a nicer shape " (B7) ; " the one I like best is D, because you can't notice it " (B7) ; " I like fish to eat, and it is a nice clean picture " (B6).

E preferred, because " the scenery is so well fitted in " (G12).

G preferred, because " I do like the shape " (B7) ; " has a better pattern, is neater " (G10) ; " is a nicer pattern " (G6).

The following results are not shown on the graph as the number of people tested is so small in each instance that the average quoted is not to be relied upon. They are given here as suggestive only.

The twenty-four children (and their teachers) of a remote village school in Swaledale, Yorkshire, 12 per cent. of right choices.

Thirty members of the Don Corsack choir (tested to see if a sense of rhythm in song led to a sense of rhythm in painting), 34 per cent. of right choices.

English Mission school in Pemba, Zanzibar (Swahili, Arabs, and Indians). Sixteen men and women in touch with the school, but most of them unable to read or write, 48 per cent. of right choices.

Six small boys, aged 5–7, attending school (?), 54 per cent. of right choices.

Thirty-nine boys, aged 10–17, attending school (where a few English and European pictures and illustrated papers were to be seen), 27 per cent. of right choices.

The amusing thing about the answers of these boys was that the greater number of them stated that they preferred A to B, because of some such reasons as the following :

" I choose A because it is of a very beautiful woman and she is in very good health. She and her child also are well dressed. If a man is well clothed he is more pleasing than a dirty man. And if a man is dirty he is very much disliked " (12 years).

" I have chosen A because it is very finely clad and if a person is finely clad he is pleasing to every one, and a person who is well clothed is pleasing to God " (17 years).

" I have chosen A because it is fine and she baths herself and her son ; also they are in a well-kept place, they are eating good food, the dirt is taken away from near their house ; people like this are much loved, and if a man is dirty he is not liked " (14 years).

" I like A because it is smart and looks healthy. She baths herself and makes her child bath. Her condition is good, and so I like her. Perhaps the other one keeps herself dirty and also her child, and so I do not like her " (14 years).

" Because she keeps herself well and moves to and fro in the fresh air " (12 years).

On inquiry it turned out that the boys were having a course of lessons on hygiene. These lessons were no doubt very necessary, but it is obvious that the æsthetic sense had not a chance when in competition with the desire to propitiate those in authority and the wish to show off knowledge. And this is not only true in Africa.

In their comments upon the other illustrations the boys' answers differed little from those of European children. It may be added that experts state that to test natives who have received no education would be an impossibility. They would be unable to compare and judge the different illustrations.

In conclusion, I would like to give my warm thanks to all those teachers who, in spite of their own heavy work, undertook the extra labour of testing the children in their charge   I am still anxious to hear of people who would be willing to give the test, or arrange for it to be given, in other parts of the world, in particular in the East and in places where taste is not yet corrupted.

July 1925   M. H. B.

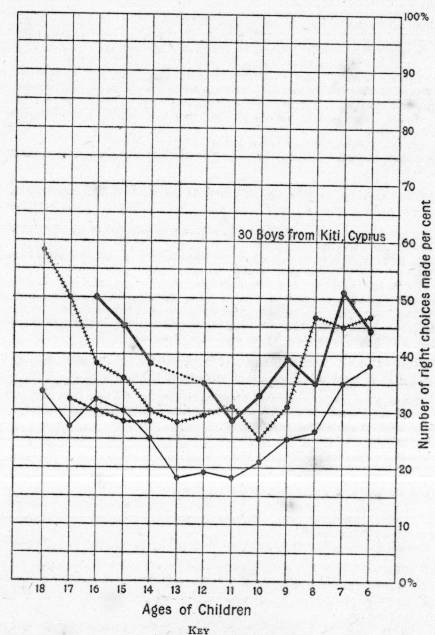

Ages of Children

KEY

317 boys and girls from elementary schools in Nicosia, Cyprus (few children of 13, 17, or 18 were tested)   ▬▬▬▬▬▬

1015 French boys and girls (chiefly girls) from the Écoles Élémentaires, degrés Inférieures et Supérieures ; 728 from Marseilles, Toulouse, and villages in the Bouches du Rhone ; 287 from Havre   .   +++++++++++++++

2038 girls and boys from English elementary schools, continuation schools, and clubs   .   .   ——————

108 Japanese girls attending Y.W.C.A. school in Tokio .   .   .   .   ▪-▪-▪-▪-▪-▪-▪-▪-▪-

APPENDIX II

LIST OF QUOTATIONS AND THEIR SOURCES

(When a quotation has been made up from passages taken from different chapters or parts of a book or from different works by the same author, a small space has been left between such passages. Their sources can be found by reference to the number of the quotation in the following list.)

CHAPTER I

Art and Imitation

1. GOETHE . . . . *Goethe's Literary Essays.* Edited Springarn, 53–7. Oxford University Press.
2. TOLSTOY . . . . *What is Art?* Trans. A. Maude, 111. Walter Scott Publishing Co.
3. BAUDELAIRE . . . *Curiosités Esthetiques,* 258–264. Calman Lévy.
4. RUSKIN . . . . *Stones of Venice,* iii. 201–204 ; vol. 11, Library Edition. George Allen.
    " . . . . *Modern Painters,* iii. 81, 186 ; vol. 5, Library Edition. George Allen.
5. DELACROIX . . . See *L'Art Romantique,* Baudelaire, 10–13. Calman Lévy.
6. WHISTLER . . . *Ten o'Clock,* 14. Chatto & Windus.
7. WILLIAM BLAKE . . *Descriptive Catalogue No. 4: The Bard, from Gray.*
    " . *A Vision of the Last Judgement.*
    " . *Public Addresses: Chaucer's Canterbury Pilgrims.*
8. CÉZANNE . . . . *Cézanne,* A. Vollard, 14. Crès.
    " . . . . *Cézanne,* J. Gasquet, 80–82, 107, 123. Berneim Jeune.
9. MAILLOL . . . . *Aristide Maillol,* Alfred Kuhn, 12–14. Seemann.
10. COLERIDGE . . . *Biographia Literaria.* Edited Shawcross, ii. 257–258. Clarendon Press.
11. CHING HAO . . . *An Introduction to the Study of Chinese Painting,* A. Waley, 169–170. Benn.
12. INGRES . . . . *Pensées,* 120–123, 72, 105. Editions de la Sirène.
13. SIR JOSHUA REYNOLDS . See *Art of Painting,* Du Fresnoy, 68. Ward.
14. GOETHE . . . . *Conversations of Goethe with Eckermann,* i. 399–401. Smith Elder.

CHAPTER II

Design

15. SHELLEY . . . . *Prometheus Unbound.*
16. WILLIAM BLAKE . . *On Homer's Poetry* (title page).
17. J. GWYN . . . . *An Essay on Design,* i–iv.
18. GEORGIO VASARI . . *Vasari on Technique.* Trans. Maclehose, 205, 284. Dent.
19. LAURENCE BINYON . . *The Art of Asia.* Reprinted from "Transactions of Japan Society of London," vol. xiv. 13–14.
20. GOETHE . . . . *Conversations of Goethe with Eckermann,* i. 394. Smith Elder.
21. C. J. HOLMES . . . *Notes on the Science of Picture-Making,* 23. Chatto & Windus.
22. LEONE BAPTISTA ALBERTI . *The Architecture of Leone Baptista Alberti.* Trans. Leoni, Book VI. chap. ii. 113 ; Book I. chap. ix. 14 ; Book IX. chap. v. 194.
23. RUSKIN . . . . *Modern Painters,* v. 208–210 ; vol. 7, Library Edition. George Allen.

93

23. RUSKIN . . . . . *Modern Painters*, v. 214–215 ; vol. **7**, Library Edition. George Allen.
   ,, ... *The Two Paths*, 334–335 ; vol. **16**, Library Edition. George Allen.
   ,, ... *The Study of Architecture*, 35 ; vol. **19**, Library Edition. George Allen.
   ,, ... *Modern Painters*, iii. 121–122 ; vol. **5**, Library Edition. George Allen.
24. DELACROIX . . . *Études Esthetiques*, 63–64. Crès.
   ,, . . . *Journal d'Eugène Delacroix*, ii. 336–338, 343. Librairie Plon.
25. COLERIDGE . . . *Biographia Literaria*. Edited Shawcross, ii. 238–239. Clarendon Press.
26. GOETHE . . . *Conversations of Goethe with Eckermann*, i. 82–83. Smith Elder.
27. SCHILLER . . . *Schiller's Philosophical Letters and Essays*. Trans. Weis, 135–136. Chapman.
28. BERNARD BERENSON . . *The Florentine Painters of the Renaissance*, 9–11, 35–36. Putnam.
29. ROGER FRY . . . *Vision and Design*, 124–125. Chatto & Windus.
30. CROCE . . . *Æsthetic*. Trans. Ainslie, 180–181. Macmillan.
31. WILLIAM JAMES . . . *Letters of William James*, ii. 86–87. Longmans.
32. TCHEKHOV . . . *Life and Letters of Anton Tchehov*. Trans. Koteliansky and Tomlinson, 129–130. Cassell.
33. RENOIR . . . *Renoir*, Albert André, 37. Crès.
34. BAUDELAIRE . . . *L'Art Romantique*, 230. Calman Lévy.
35. COLERIDGE . . . *Biographia Literaria*. Edited Shawcross, ii. 65. Clarendon Press.
36. SHELLEY . . . *The Defence of Poetry*.
37. RUSKIN . . . *Various Addresses*, 474 ; vol. **16**, Library Edition. George Allen.
38. DELACROIX . . . *Journal d'Eugène Delacroix*, ii. 241. Librairie Plon.
39. ROBERT BRIDGES . . *The Necessity of Poetry*, 39. Oxford University Press.
40. SIR WILLIAM TEMPLE . *Essays on Learning and on Poetry*. Edited Springarn, 50–51. Clarendon Press.

CHAPTER III

ANALYSIS OF DESIGN (*a*)

41. FROEBEL . . . *Education by Development*, 59, 204–317. Arnold.
   ,, . . . *Pedagogics of the Kindergarten*, 92–97. Appleton.
42. CAMPBELL AND GARNETT . *Life of James Clerk-Maxwell*, 38. Macmillan.
43. PASCAL . . . *Pensées*.
44. ALBRECHT DÜRER . . *The Literary Remains of Albrecht Dürer*, W. M. Conway, 165. Cambridge University Press.
45. SIR CHRISTOPHER WREN . *Parentalia*, C. Wren, 237. Arnold.
46. RODIN . . . *The Life and Works of Auguste Rodin*, F. Lawton, 157, 162. Fisher Unwin.
47. SCHILLER . . . *Schiller's Philosophical Letters and Essays*. Trans. Weis, 293. Chapman.
48. PATER . . . *Plato and Platonism*, 272. Macmillan.
49. ROGER FRY . . . *Architectural Heresies of a Painter*, 25–30. Chatto & Windus.
50. SCHOPENHAUER . . . *Works*. Trans. Haldane and Kemp, iii. 186–188 ; i. 277–279. Trübner.
51. BERNARD BERENSON . . *The Florentine Painters of the Renaissance*, 3–4, 12. Putnam.
52. A. VOLLARD . . . *Cézanne*, 155–156. Crès.
53. CÉZANNE . . . *Cézanne*, J. Gasquet, 89. Berneim Jeune.
54. CROCE . . . *Æsthetic*. Trans. Ainslie, 174–175. Macmillan.

CHAPTER IV

ANALYSIS OF DESIGN (*b*)

55. ROGER FRY . . . *Vision and Design*, 22–25. Chatto & Windus.
56. WILLIAM BLAKE . . *Public Addresses : Chaucer's Canterbury Pilgrims*.

57. RUSKIN . . . . . *Modern Painters*, iv. 72 ; vol. **6**, Library Edition. George Allen.
58. BAUDELAIRE . . . . *Curiosités Esthetiques*, 94, 272. Calman Lévy.
59. INGRES . . . . *Pensées*, 90. Editions de la Sirène.

CHAPTER V

ANALYSIS OF DESIGN (*c*)

60. RUSKIN . . . . *Stones of Venice*, ii. 215–221 ; vol. **10**, Library Edition. George Allen.
61. BERNARD BERENSON . . *The Central Italian Painters of the Renaissance*, 5–14. Putnam.
62. ROGER FRY . . . See *Burlington Magazine*, Sept. 1922.
63. C. J. HOLMES . . *Notes on the Science of Picture-Making*, 15–16. Chatto & Windus.
64. JOHN CROME . . *Collins Baker*, 63–64. Methuen.
65. ROGER FRY . . . *A Sampler of Castille*, 70–71. The Hogarth Press.
66. BERNARD BERENSON . . *The Central Italian Painters of the Renaissance*, 96–99. Putnam.
67. ROGER FRY . . . *Vision and Design*, 20–22. Chatto & Windus.
68. NIETZSCHE . . . *Works*. Edited Levy, x. 117–119. Foulis.
69. LAURENCE BINYON . . *The Flight of the Dragon* (Wisdom of the East Series), 14–19. Murray.
70. GOETHE . . . . *Conversations of Goethe with Eckermann*, ii. 162. Smith Elder.
    „ . . . . *Goethe's Opinions*. Trans. Wenckstern, 114. John Parker.
71. COLERIDGE . . . *Biographia Literaria*. Edited Shawcross, ii. 49, 53, 55–56. Clarendon Press.
72. ROBERT BRIDGES . . *The Necessity of Poetry*, 29–30. Clarendon Press.
73. CROCE . . . . *The Essence of Æsthetic*. Trans. Ainslie, 39–41. Heinemann.
74. RÉMY DE GOURMONT . *Promenades Littéraires*, 18. Mercure de France.
75. SCHOPENHAUER . . *Works*. Trans. Haldane and Kemp, i. 331–336. Trübner.
76. DELACROIX . . . *Le Journal d'Eugène Delacroix*, ii. 223. Librairie Plon.
77. FLAUBERT . . . See translation by Pater, *Appreciations*, 30. Macmillan.
78. COLERIDGE . . . *Biographia Literaria*. Edited Shawcross, ii. 258–259, 262. Clarendon Press.
79. DE QUINCEY . . . *Works*. Edited Masson, x. 262. A. & C. Black.
80. BAUDELAIRE . . . *L'Art Romantique*, 54–55. Calman Lévy.
81. SHELLEY . . . . *The Defence of Poetry*.
82. GOETHE . . . . *Goethe's Literary Essays*. Edited Springarn, 22. Oxford University Press.
83. LASCELLES ABERCROMBIE . *An Essay towards a Theory of Art*, 101–109. Secker.
84. CHEHOV (TCHEKHOV) . . See *Anton Chehov*, W. Gerhardi, 17. Cobden Sanderson.
85. FRANCIS BACON . . *Works*. Edited Spedding, Ellis, and Heath, IV. "De Augmentis," 292, 315–316 ; III. "The Advancement of Learning," 343–344.
86. MICHAEL ANGELO BUONARROTI . *Selected Poems from Michael Angelo Buonarrotti*. Edited Chesney, 101 (Wordsworth's translation). Lee & Shepherd.
87. EINSTEIN . . . . See *The Dance of Life*, Havelock Ellis, 126–127. Constable.
88. SHELLEY . . . . *The Defence of Poetry*.
89. GOETHE . . . . *The Letters of Goethe to Zelter*. Trans. Coleridge, 293. Bell.
90. SIR THOMAS BROWNE . *Religio Medici*. Edition of 1642, ii.
91. GEORGE SANTAYANA . *Interpretations of Poetry and Religion*, 269–270. Constable.

CHAPTER VI

TASTE AND THE APPRECIATION OF ART

92. WILLIAM BLAKE . . *There is no Natural Religion*.
    „ . . . *A Vision of the Last Judgment*.

93. COLERIDGE . . . . *Biographia Literaria*. Edited Shawcross, ii. 227, 229–230. Clarendon Press.

94. WORDSWORTH . . . *Essay Supplementary to Preface to Lyrical Ballads*.

95. ROBERT BRIDGES . . *The Necessity of Poetry*, 5. Oxford University Press.

96. RUSKIN . . . . *The Two Paths*, 296 ; vol. 16, Library Edition. George Allen.

97. T. S. ELIOT . . . *The Sacred Wood*, 44–49. Methuen.

98. SCHOPENHAUER . . *Works*. Trans. Haldane and Kemp, iii. 177–180. Trübner.

99. RUSKIN . . . . *Stones of Venice*, iii. 212–215 ; vol. 11, Library Edition. George Allen.

100. COLERIDGE . . . *Biographia Literaria*. Edited Shawcross, 242–243. Clarendon Press.

101. CÉZANNE . . . . *Cézanne*, J. Gasquet, 101–104. Berneim Jeune.

102. WILLIAM JAMES . . *Elements of Psychology*, ii. 471–472. Holt.

103. MICHAEL ANGELO BUONARROTI *Michael Angelo Buonarroti*, Holroyd, 280. Duckworth.

104. SIR JOSHUA REYNOLDS . *The Discourses of Sir Joshua Reynolds*, xiii.

105. GEORGE MOORE . . *Modern Painters*, 150. Walter Scott Publishing Co.

106. RUSKIN . . . . *Stones of Venice*, ii. 434–436 ; vol. 10, Library Edition. George Allen.

107. SCHOPENHAUER . . *Works*. Trans. Haldane and Kemp, iii. 201.

108. GEORGE BERNARD SHAW . See *Saturday Review*, 11th April 1896.

109. BAUDELAIRE . . . *Curiosités Esthetiques*, 212–213. Calman Lévy.

110. TOLSTOY . . . . *What is Art ?* Trans. A. Maude, 143–146. Walter Scott Publishing Co.

111. C. J. HOLMES . . . *Notes on the Science of Picture-Making*, 283, 297–298. Chatto & Windus.

112. As given.

113. As given.

114. CHRISTOPHER WREN (quoted by) . *Parentalia*, 120–121. Arnold.

115. GEORGE BERNARD SHAW . *Three Plays for Puritans* (" Cæsar and Cleopatra "), 196. Constable.

116. SHELLEY . . . . *The Defence of Poetry*.

CHAPTER VII

The Relation of Art to Religion, Morality, and the Spiritual Life

117. A. CLUTTON BROCK . . *The Ultimate Belief*, 19–101. Constable.

118. ROGER FRY . . . *Vision and Design*, 14–15, 36, 47, 199. Chatto & Windus.

119. RUSKIN . . . . *Modern Painters*, v. 264 ; vol. 7, Library Edition. George Allen.

120. RABELAIS . . . . *Pantagruel*, Book III. chap. xxxi.

121. SHELLEY . . . . *The Defence of Poetry*.

122. GEORGE SANTAYANA . *The Sense of Beauty*, 65, 264. Constable.

123. DE QUINCEY . . . *Works*. Edited Masson, xi. 173. A. & C. Black.

124. RUSKIN . . . . *Lectures on Art*, 93 ; vol. 20, Library Edition. George Allen.

125. RENAN . . . . *Feuilles Detachées*, 345. Lévy.

126. CROCE . . . . *The Essence of Æsthetic*. Trans. Ainslie, 14, 73–74, 77. Heinemann.

„ . . . . *Æsthetic*. Trans. Ainslie, 84–87. Macmillan.

127. RUSKIN . . . . *Modern Painters*, ii. 387–389 ; vol. 4, Library Edition. George Allen.

128. CHARLES DARWIN . . *The Life of Charles Darwin*. Edited F. Darwin, i. 100–102. Murray.

129. WILLIAM BLAKE . . *Jerusalem*.

„ . . . . *A Vision of the Last Judgment*.

130. GOETHE . . . . *Goethe's Opinions*. Trans. Wenckstern, 82. John Parker.

131. LYTTON STRACHEY . . *Books and Characters*, 11. Chatto & Windus.

132. GOETHE . . . . *Goethe's Conversations with Eckermann*, ii. 425. Smith Elder.

APPENDIX III

LIST OF ILLUSTRATIONS, ATTRIBUTIONS, AND SOURCES

FRONTISPIECE (see CHAPTER II)

1. DRAWING OF A SHEET. By a Girl (aged 15) from Nicosia, Cyprus. Collection of Mr. Diamanti Christodoulides.
2. EVE. Bougereau.
3. SPANISH GIRL. (Photo, J. Hope-Johnstone.)
4. PORTRAIT OF A GIRL. Vermeer of Delft, Hague. (Photo, Bruckmann.)

CHAPTER I

ART AND IMITATION

5. THE LADIES' WALK, WREST PARK. (Photo, *Country Life*.)
6. PHOTOGRAPH OF THE PIAZZA DI SAN MARCO, VENICE. (Photo, Brogi.)
7. PAINTING OF THE PIAZZA DI SAN MARCO, VENICE. School of Guardi. Victoria and Albert Museum, South Kensington.
8. PHOTOGRAPH OF THE COLOSSEUM, ROME. (Photo, Alinari.)
9. PAINTING OF THE COLOSSEUM, ROME. Corot. (Photo, Druet.)
10. PHOTOGRAPH OF A SCENE IN JAPAN.
11. JAPANESE COLOUR PRINT OF SAME SCENE. Hiroshige.
12. PHOTOGRAPH OF SEATED FIGURE. (Photo, J. Hope-Johnstone.)
13. SKETCH OF SAME SITTER. Walter Sickert, A.R.A. From the Collection of Mrs. R. R. Tatlock.
14. STILL LIFE. (Photo, J. Hope-Johnstone.)
15. STILL LIFE. Cézanne. (Photo, Druet.)
16. ALEXANDRE DUMAS. Attributed to Daumier.
17. PHOTOGRAPH OF DUMAS.
18. LITHOGRAPH OF DUMAS.
19. PORTRAIT BUST. By courtesy of The Cameograph Photo-Sculpture Ltd.
20. HEAD OF GATAMALATA (detail). Donatello. Padua. (Photo, Alinari.)
21. BUST OF ACKHNATON, KING OF EGYPT. *c.* 1350 B.C. Louvre. (Photo, Giraudon.)
22. BUST OF MEMBER OF THE CAPPONI FAMILY. Florentine. Early Sixteenth Century. (From a death mask.) Victoria and Albert Museum, South Kensington.
23. THE WRESTLERS. (Photo, Hill.)
24. LA RIXE. Engraving after Meisonnier. (Photo, Mansell.)
25. HERCULES AND ANTÆUS. Antonio Pollaiuolo. Uffizi, Florence. (Photo, Alinari.)
26. CAIN AND ABEL. Tintoretto. Academy, Venice. (Photo, Alinari.)
27. HORSEMEN FROM PARTHENON FRIEZE. Fifth Century B.C. British Museum. (Photo, Mansell.)
28. STREET SCENE. By a Girl (aged 16) from the High School, Dudley. Collection of Miss Marion Richardson.
29. SACRED AND PROFANE LOVE. Titian. Borghese Gallery, Rome. (Photo, Alinari.)
30. DRAWINGS OF CARVINGS, ETC., BY NATIVES OF SOLOMON ISLANDS. From article by Mr. H. Balfour, M.A., *Man*, June 1905.
31. LANDSCAPE. Henri-Matisse. (Photo, Berneim Jeune.)

7

32. ROARING TIGER. Chinese. Yuan Dynasty (A.D. 1280–1368). From *Animaux dans l'art chinois*. Ardennes de Tizac. A. Lévy.
33. LANDSCAPE. Pencil Drawing. Constable. Victoria and Albert Museum, South Kensington.
34. PORTRAIT OF A CARDINAL. Raphael. Prado, Madrid. (Photo, Roig.)

CHAPTER II

DESIGN

35. SACRIFICIAL BOWL WITH FRIEZE OF SKULLS. Nazca. Ancient Peru. From *The Art of Old Peru*, W. Lehmann. Benn.
36. BOWL. Modern. From a water-colour.
37. BOWL CUT FROM AN AGATE. Roman (?). Treasury of San Marco, Venice. (Photo, Alinari.)
38. CHRIST IN THE HOUSE OF HIS PARENTS. J. E. Millais. Tate Gallery.
39. PIÉTA. School of Nicholas Froment (?) 1470 (?) Louvre. (Photo, Giraudon.)
40. SKETCH FOR " ENTRY INTO A PORT." Claude Lorrain. École des Beaux Arts, Paris.
41. OIL PAINTING, " ENTRY INTO A PORT." Claude Lorrain. Dulwich Gallery. (Photo, Hanfstaengl.)
42. SKETCH FOR " THE MASSACRE OF THE INNOCENTS." Poussin. Chantilly.
43. OIL PAINTING, " THE MASSACRE OF THE INNOCENTS." Poussin. Chantilly.

CHAPTER III

ANALYSIS OF DESIGN (a)

44. AMERICAN GRAIN ELEVATOR.
45. ABBAYE AUX DAMES. Caen. (Photo, Neurdein.)
46. PYRAMID OF CAIUS CESTIUS AND PORTA OSTIENSIS, ROME. (Photo, Alinari.)
47. TITHE BARN. Bradford-on-Avon. (Photo, *Country Life*.)
48. ST. PAUL'S CATHEDRAL. (Sir Christopher Wren's favourite model.) (Photo, *Artists Illustrators*.)
49. THE HOSPITAL, CORSHAM. (Photo, *Country Life*.)
50. ROMAN TOMB (" LA CONOCCHIA "). Santa Maria, Capua Vetere. Second Century A.D. From *Moslem Architecture*, Rivoira. Oxford University Press.
51. CHINESE BOWL. Sung Dynasty (A.D. 960–1280). Collection of Mr. George Eumorfopoulos.
52. A CONVERSATION. Negro Sculpture from Congo. From *Negerplastik*, C. Einstein. Kurt Wolff.
53. CHINESE VASE. Sung Dynasty (A.D. 960–1280).
54. JOAN OF ARC. Chapu. Orleans. (Photo, Neurdein.)
55. THE KNUCKLEBONE PLAYER. Greek (Tanagra). Fourth to Third Century B.C. British Museum.

CHAPTER IV

ANALYSIS OF DESIGN (b)

56. CHINESE SCRIPT. Attributed to Confucius. From *An Introduction to the Study of Chinese Painting*, A. D. Waley. Benn.
57. CHINESE SCRIPT. T'ang copy of Fourth Century original. From *The Kokka*, November 1908.
58. PERSIAN BOWL. From Rakka. Thirteenth Century.
59. WINDSOR CHAIR. c. 1710. From Lenygon's *Furniture in England*. B. T. Batsford Ltd.
60. HOT WATER URN. English. Eighteenth Century.
61. STUDY FOR HEAD OF ST. CATHERINE. Raphael. From *Drawings of Old Masters in University Galleries, Oxford*, vol. ii., Sidney Colvin. Oxford University Press.
62. STUDY FOR THE HAMAN (Sistine Chapel). Michael Angelo. British Museum.
63. LION. Chinese. Ninth Century (?). From Tun-Huang. Stein Collection, British Museum.

64. THE BIRTH OF VENUS. Botticelli. Uffizzi, Florence. (Photo, Alinari.)
65. ACQUA PAULA. Rome. Sixteenth Century. (Photo, Alinari.)
66. STONE CARVING. From Mosque of Aljaferia. Museum, Saragossa. (Photo, Laurent.)
67. JADE TOAD. Chinese. Shang Dynasty (?) (1760–1122 B.C.). Collection of Mrs. Pope-Hennessy.
68. MEDIÆVAL CROSS. c. 850. Lateran, Rome. From *Monuments et Memoires* (Fondation Piot), 1907, vol. XV.
69. OLD HOUSES. South side of street, Guildford. (Photo, Frith.)
70. MODERN HOUSES. North side of same street, Guildford. (Photo, by permission of Heath & Salter.)
71. ADORATION OF MAGI. Giotto. Arena Chapel, Padua. (Photo, Alinari.)
72. PORTRAIT OF MISS GERTRUDE STEIN. Picasso. Collection of Miss Stein. (Photo, Giraudon.)
73. JAR OF FLOWERS. Cézanne. (Photo, Druet.)
74. ANNUNCIATION. Overbeck. (Photo, Mansell.)
75. ANNUNCIATION. Fra Angelico. Convent of San Marco, Florence. (Photo, Alinari.)
76. INTERIOR OF CHURCH OF ST. FRONT, PÉRIGUEUX. 984–1047. (Photo, *Archives Photographiques d'Art et d'Histoire*.)
77. LANDSCAPE. Guardi. From album of drawings. See *Francesco Guardi*, G. A. Simonson. Methuen.
78. LANDSCAPE. Guardi. From album of drawings.

CHAPTER V

ANALYSIS OF DESIGN (c)

79. OLD EMBROIDERED DANCING DRESS. Bu-Shongo tribe, Congo State. British Museum.
80. RELIEF. Modena Cathedral. Early Twelfth Century (?). (Photo, Orlandini.)
81. STILL LIFE. William Hunt.
82. STILL LIFE. Chardin. Louvre. (Photo, Giraudon.)
83. VENUS. Titian. Bridgewater House. (Photo, Mansell.)
84. THE RESURRECTION. Piero della Francesca. Borgo San Sepolcro. (Photo, Alinari.)
85. TATTOOED WOMAN. New Guinea. (Photo, Captain Barton.)
86. MAYA NUMERALS. Detail from cast of Stele, Copan (c. 153 A.D.). British Museum.
87. CAPITAL OF COLUMN. Church of St. Lazare, Autun. Twelfth Century. (Photo, *Archives Photographiques d'Art et d'Histoire*.)
88. RELIEF. Cathedral, Modena. Early Twelfth Century (?). (Photo, Orlandini.)
89. SNOWY LANDSCAPE. Chinese. Attributed to Yang Fei. End of Eighth Century. From *An Introduction to the Study of Chinese Painting*, A. D. Waley. Benn.
90. PORTRAIT OF MONSIEUR GEOFFROI. Cézanne. (Photo, Druet.)
91. THE LAOCOÖN. El Greco. Pinakothek, Munich. (Photo, Hanfstaengl.)
92. THE " DISPUTA." Raphael. Vatican, Rome. (Photo, Alinari.)
93. STUDY OF TREES. Poussin. Louvre, Paris.
94. THE CONCERT. Giorgione. Louvre, Paris. (Photo, Alinari.)
95. THE ENTOMBMENT. Giotto. Arena Chapel, Padua. (Photo, Alinari.)
96. BIRD ON A BOUGH. Chinese. Sung Dynasty (A.D. 960–1280). Collection of Mr. George Eumorfopoulos.
97. DESCENT FROM THE CROSS (detail). Russian. Fifteenth Century. Formerly in Collection of Ostrooukhov.
98. LEONELLO D'ESTE. Pisanello. Morelli Gallery, Bergamo. (Photo, Alinari.)
99. IDEALISED PORTRAIT OF MARY QUEEN OF SCOTS (?) French. Sixteenth Century. National Gallery.
100. THE VISION OF ST. EUSTACE. Pisanello. National Gallery.
101. HUNTING SCENE. Paolo Ucello. Ashmolean, Oxford.
102. DANCING GIRL. Greek (Tanagra). Fourth to Third Century B.C. Bibliothèque Nationale, Paris. (Photo, Giraudon.)
103. THE DANCE OF SIVA. Indian. Twelfth Century (?). Museum, Madras. (Photo Collection Goloubew, Musée Guimet, Paris.)
104. THE FLAYED OX. Rembrandt. Louvre. (Photo, Neurdein.)

105. THE EAVES-DROPPER. William Hunt. From *Ruskin on Pictures*, ii. Allen & Unwin.
106. THE YELLOW CHAIR. Van Gogh. Tate Gallery.
107. ANDROMEDA. Rembrandt. Collection of Dr. Bredius, Hague.
108. CHINESE BOWL. Sung Dynasty. Collection of Mr. George Eumorfopoulos.
109. CHINESE BOWL. Sung Dynasty. Collection of Mr. George Eumorfopoulos.
110. PRE-HISTORIC BOWL. Maidstone Museum.
111. MODERN VASES.
112. MODERN TEAPOT.
113. MODERN TEAPOT. (Omega Workshops.)
114. BRIDGES. Carstal. Garabit. (Photo, *Archives Photographiques d'Art et d'Histoire*.)
115. THE TERRACE, WILTON. (Photo, *Country Life*.)
116. ROLLS-ROYCE CAR. (By permission.)
117. GOLDEN COACH OF QUEEN OF HOLLAND. From *Album of Illustrations of Imperial and Royal State and other Coaches*, published by The Worshipful Company of Coach Makers, 1899.
118. HEAD OF AN ATHLETE. Greek. *c.* 472 B.C. Athens. (Photo, Alinari.)
119. HEAD OF A CHARIOTEER (detail). Greek. *c.* 480 to 450 B.C. Delphi. (Photo, Alinari.)
120. HEAD OF HERMES (detail). Praxiteles. Active 370 to 350 B.C. Olympia. (Photo, Mansell.)
121. HEAD OF AGIAS (detail). Lycippus. Active *c.* 330 to 315 B.C.

CHAPTER VI

TASTE AND THE APPRECIATION OF ART

122. BASKET OF FLOWERS. Line drawing. Modern.
123. BASKET OF FLOWERS. Old woodcut. From *Embroidery*, Part I., James Pearsal.
124. EMBROIDERED BORDER. Modern.
125. EMBROIDERED BORDER. Eighteenth Century. From Crete. Victoria and Albert Museum, South Kensington.
126. STAINED GLASS, METHUSELAH. Twelfth Century. Canterbury Cathedral. From water-colour by L. Saint. Victoria and Albert Museum, South Kensington.
127. STAINED GLASS. Modern. From Cartoon. (Photo, J. Wippell & Co.)
128. LETTERING. Twentieth Century. (Photo, Roneo.)
129. LETTERING. Eighteenth and Nineteenth Centuries. Whitefield's Tabernacle.
130. SETTEE. English. 1898. From a drawing.
131. ARM-CHAIR. Sheriton (?). Soane Museum.
132. CHAIR FROM SAME SET. Soane Museum.
133. SETTEE. English. *c.* 1730. Collection of Duke of Hamilton. (Photo, *Country Life*.)
134. TOWN HALL, LOUVAIN. 1448–1463. (Photo, Nels.)
135. TOWN HALL, STOCKHOLM. Modern. R. Ostberg. (Photo, Hernlin.)
136. BAPTISTRY, TRAU. Alessi. 1467.
137. INTERIOR OF ROOM. French. *c.* 1900.
138. DOORWAY, CHURCH OF THE MADELEINE, VEZELAY. Twelfth Century. (Photo, Neurdein.)
139. DOORWAY. Modern. Czecho-Slovakia.
140. NETHER LYPIATT. Cotswolds (1702–1705). (Photo, *Country Life*.)
141. "ART NOUVEAU" HOUSE. French. *c.* 1900.
142. PRAYING MONK. Chinese. T'ang Dynasty (618–907 A.D.).
143. SAINT IN PRAYER. Japanese. British Museum.
144. CHRIST THE CONSOLER. James F. Forsyth. St. Paul's Cathedral.
145. CHRIST OF THE APOCALYPSE. Chartres Cathedral. Twelfth Century. (Photo, Houvet.)
146. WOUNDED AMAZON. Professor Friedrich.
147. SEATED WOMAN. Maillol. (Photo, Druet.)
148. NAPIR-ASU, WIFE OF KING OF ELAM (?). *c.* 1500 B.C. From Susa. Louvre. (Photo, Giraudon.)

149. QUEEN VICTORIA. Imperial Institute. (Photo, Frith.)
150. BUST OF GIRL. Cast bronze. Sixteenth Century. From Benin City, Southern Nigeria. British Museum.
151. MADAME LYDIA LOPOKHOVA. Frank Dobson.
152. BUST OF GIRL. Nineteenth Century.
153. REVERIE. Sir Frank Dicksee, P.R.A. Walker Art Gallery, Liverpool. (Photo, Mansell.)
154. AT THE PIANO. Whistler. Collection of Edmund Davis.
155. BATHERS (ACTEON AND DIANA). Titian. Bridgewater House. (Photo, Mansell.)
156. BATHERS. Borgereau. (Photo, Knoedler.)
157. BATHERS. Renoir.
158. CASTOR AND POLLUX. Pen and wash drawing. Poussin. Chantilly.
159. BACCHUS AND SILENE. Fesco from Bos Coreale, near Pompeii. c. 50–60 A.D. British Museum.
160. THE INFANTA MARIA THERESA. Velasquez. Prado. (Photo, Roig.)
161. THE DUCHESSE D'AUMALE. Winterhalter. Versailles. (Photo, Neurdein.)
162. THE FALLEN IDOL. The Hon. John Collier, R.A. (Photo, Autotype Co.)
163. JOHN ARNOLFINI AND HIS WIFE. Jan Van Eyck. National Gallery.
164. THE VISITATION. Giotto. Arena Chapel, Padua. (Photo, Alinari.)
165. ARRIVAL OF RELATIONS OF ST. GIULLANO (detail). Gardner Hale. Villa Razzollini, Florence. (Photo, Brogi.)
166. MADONNA AND CHILD (detail). Raphael. Dresden. (Photo, Hanfstaengl.)
167. THE LADY OF THE LILIES. A. E. MacIntosh. (By permission of Messrs. Mowbray.)
168. SCENE IN A PARK (THE MALL). Gainsborough. Frick Collection, New York.
169. SCENE IN A PARK (" Who can this be ? "). C. R. Leslie. Victoria and Albert Museum, South Kensington.
170. SCENE IN A PARK (" La Grande Jatte "). Seurat.
171. MOUNTAIN PEAKS (near Dogelly). Paul Sandby Munn. British Museum.
172. MOUNTAIN PEAKS (detail from landscape roll). Ma Yuan (?) Sung Dynasty (A.D. 960–1280). Freer Collection, Washington, U.S.A.
173. THE VALLEY OF THE LLUGWY. W. B. Leader. Tate Gallery. (Photo, Mansell.)
174. THE THREE TREES. Etching. Rembrandt. British Museum.
175. LANDSCAPE. Oil. Modern.
176. MALVERN HALL. Constable. National Gallery.
177. STREET SCENE. By a Child (aged 15) from Nicosia, Cyprus. Collection of Mr. Diamanti Christodoulides.
178. STREET SCENE (" CAPRI "). Sir Edward Poynter, late P.R.A. From *Drawings of Sir E. Poynter*, M. Bell. Newnes.
179. LANDSCAPE NEAR AIX. Cézanne.
180. A MILL WEIR, SERRA VALLE (detail). Henry Woods.

APPENDIX

A (181). MADONNA AND CHILD. Modern.
B (182). MADONNA AND CHILD. Mantegna. Kaiser Friedrich Museum, Berlin.
C (183). PEACOCKS, AFFRONTED. Modern.
D (184). PEACOCKS, AFFRONTED. Byzantine textile. Cluny, Paris.
E (185). STUDY OF TREES. Claude Lorrain. British Museum.
F (186). AN EVENING HOUR. W. B. Leader. (Photo, The Autotype Co.)
G (187). PERSIAN MINIATURE. (Photo, Druet.)
H (188). MODERN DISTORTION OF THE SAME.

PRINTED BY MORRISON AND GIBB LTD., EDINBURGH

PLATE II

Fig. 5

Fig. 6

Fig. 7

PLATE III

Fig. 10

Fig. 11

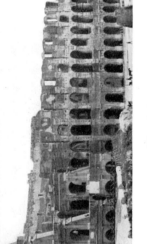

Fig. 8

Fig. 9

PLATE IV

Fig. 12

Fig. 13

Fig. 14

Fig. 15

PLATE V

Fig. 16

Fig. 17

Fig. 18

PLATE VI

Fig. 19

Fig. 20

Fig. 21

Fig. 22

PLATE VII

Fig. 24

Fig. 26

Fig. 23

Fig. 25

PLATE VIII

Fig. 27

Fig. 28

Fig. 29

PLATE IX

H.Balfour del.

Fig. 30

PLATE X

Fig. 32

Fig. 34

Fig. 31

Fig. 33

PLATE XI

Fig. 36

Fig. 35

Fig. 37

Fig. 38

Fig. 39

PLATE XII

Fig. 42

Fig. 43

Fig. 40

Fig. 41

PLATE XIII

Fig. 46

Fig. 47

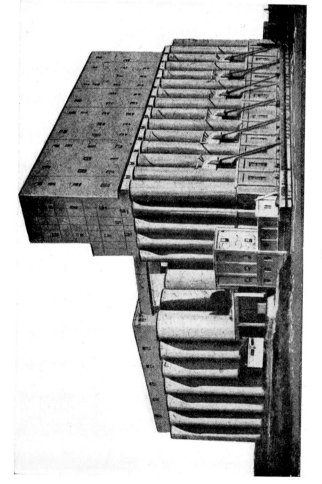

Fig. 44

Fig. 45

PLATE XIV

Fig. 48

Fig. 49

Fig. 50

PLATE XV

Fig. 51

Fig. 52

Fig. 53

Fig. 54

Fig. 55

PLATE XVI

Fig. 56

Fig. 57

Fig. 58

Fig. 59

Fig. 60

PLATE XVII

Fig. 61

Fig. 62

Fig. 63

PLATE XVIII

Fig. 64

Fig. 65

Fig. 66

PLATE XIX

Fig. 67

Fig. 68

Fig. 69

Fig. 70

PLATE XX

Fig. 71

Fig. 72

Fig. 73

PLATE XXI

Fig. 74

Fig. 75

PLATE XXII

Fig. 77

Fig. 78

Fig. 76

PLATE XXIII

Fig. 81

Fig. 82

Fig. 79

Fig. 80

PLATE XXIV

Fig. 84

Fig. 83

PLATE XXV

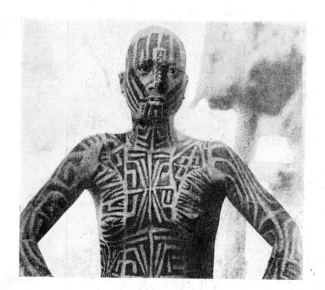

Fig. 85

Fig. 87

Fig. 86

Fig. 88

PLATE XXVI

Fig. 89

Fig. 90

Fig. 91

PLATE XXVII

Fig. 94

Fig. 92

PLATE XXVIII

Fig. 96

Fig. 97

Fig. 98

Fig. 99

PLATE XXIX

Fig. 100

Fig. 101

PLATE XXX

Fig. 103

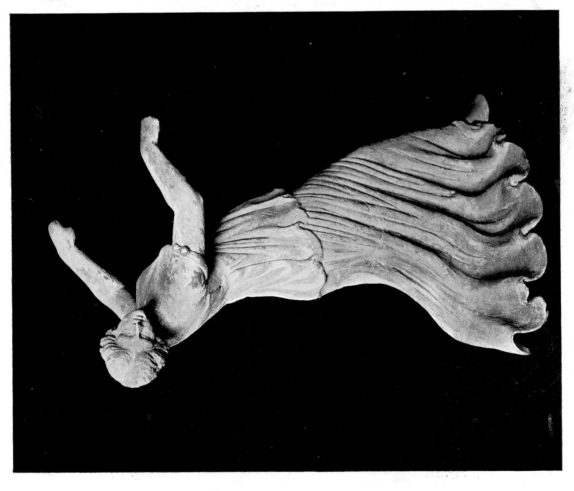

Fig. 101

PLATE XXXI

Fig. 104

Fig. 105

Fig. 106

Fig. 107

PLATE XXXII

Fig. 108

Fig. 109

Fig. 110

Fig. 111

Fig. 112

Fig. 113

PLATE XXXIII

Fig. 115

Fig. 114

Fig. 117

Fig. 116

PLATE XXXIV

Fig. 118

Fig. 119

Fig. 120

Fig 121

PLATE XXXV

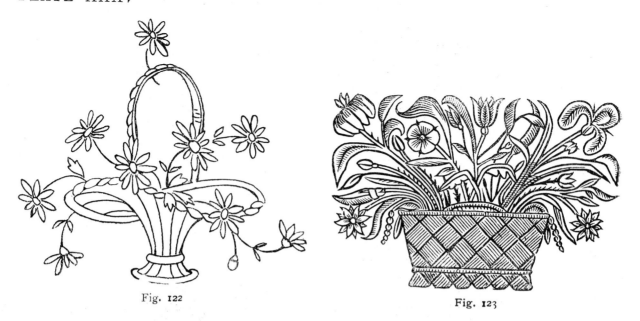

Fig. 122

Fig. 123

Fig. 124

Fig. 125

PLATE XXXVI

Fig. 126

Fig. 127

Fig. 128

Fig. 129

PLATE XXXVII

Fig. 130

Fig. 131

Fig. 132

Fig. 133

PLATE XXXVIII

Fig. 134

Fig. 135

Fig. 136

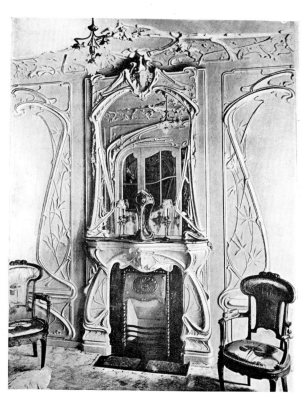

Fig. 137

PLATE XXXIX

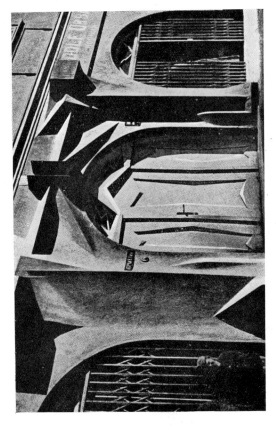

Fig. 139

Fig. 141

Fig. 138

Fig. 140

PLATE XL

Fig. 142

Fig. 143

Fig. 144

Fig. 145

PLATE XLI

Fig. 146

Fig. 147

Fig. 148

Fig. 149

PLATE XLII

Fig. 152

Fig. 154

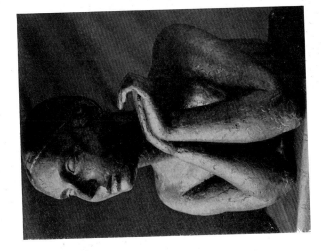

Fig. 151

Fig. 153

Fig. 150

PLATE XLIII

Fig. 155

Fig. 156

PLATE XLIV

Fig. 157

Fig. 158

Fig. 159

PLATE XLV

Fig. 160

Fig. 161

Fig. 162

Fig. 163

PLATE XLVI

Fig. 164

Fig. 165

Fig. 156

Fig. 167

PLATE XLVII

Fig. 168

Fig. 169

Fig. 170

PLATE XLVIII

Fig. 171

Fig. 172

PLATE XLIX

Fig. 175

Fig. 176

Fig. 173

Fig. 174

PLATE L

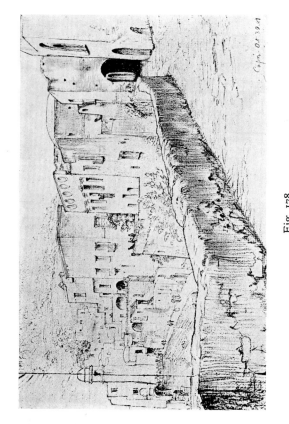

Fig. 178

Fig. 180

Fig. 179

Fig. 177

PLATE LI

A

Fig. 181

B

Fig. 182

C

Fig. 183

D

Fig. 184

PLATE LII

E

Fig. 185

F

Fig. 186

G

Fig. 187

H

Fig. 188